Consumer Directed Health Care

Consumer Directed Health Care

A 360 Degree View

Kim D. Slocum

Foreword by Ian Morrison, PhD

CRC Press
Taylor & Francis Group
Boca Raton   London   New York

CRC Press is an imprint of the
Taylor & Francis Group, an **informa** business
A PRODUCTIVITY PRESS BOOK

Productivity Press
Taylor & Francis Group
270 Madison Avenue
New York, NY 10016

© 2009 by Taylor & Francis Group, LLC
Productivity Press is an imprint of Taylor & Francis Group, an Informa business

No claim to original U.S. Government works
Printed in the United States of America on acid-free paper
10 9 8 7 6 5 4 3 2 1

International Standard Book Number-13: 978-1-56327-391-9 (Softcover)

Library of Congress Cataloging-in-Publication Data

Slocum, Kim
    Consumer directed health care : a 360 degree view / Kim D. Slocum.
      p. cm.
    Includes bibliographical references and index.
    ISBN 978-1-56327-391-9 (alk. paper)
    1. Consumer-driven health care--United States. I. Title.

RA416.5.U6S66 2008
362.1--dc22   2008006059

Visit the Taylor & Francis Web site at
http://www.taylorandfrancis.com

and the Productivity Press Web site at
http://www.productivitypress.com

To Diane

My wife, my best friend, and now my business partner.

Thanks for everything you've done all these years.

Contents

Foreword

Consumer directed health care sounds like a plausible idea. Consumers say they want control and do not just want to be passive recipients of health care, and there is the strongly held notion that if consumers were more responsible for payment for health care services they would be much more prudent in their purchasing of health insurance and health services. Couple these notions to tax-advantaged health plan designs, and you have the making of a megatrend. Well, maybe not.

First, consumers did not really ask for this type of plan. What they really wanted was broad health insurance coverage and unrestricted choice of provider, paid by someone else. But, as first-dollar insurance coverage became progressively more unaffordable to business, government, and individual households, cheaper alternatives had to be found. The easiest way to make insurance more afford-able (at least to the employer sponsor) is to raise deductibles and other forms of cost-sharing. Consumer directed health plans (CDHP) were born out of a need to find cheaper alternatives that were socially acceptable forms of cost-sharing.

Second, as this book so capably demonstrates, consumer directed health plans are a product of recent history. They were born out of the perceived failure of managed care plans to deliver consumer-acceptable value propositions, from a frustration by employers that they had few new tools to contain costs, and from the rise of an ideology of "skin in the game," that consumers should be more responsible financially for the consequences of their health care choices. Ultimately the rise of CDHP in the health policy arsenal reflects, as Kim Slocum points out, the continuing tension between the views that health care is a right like K-12 education or a privilege like any other good or service purchased by consumers. Consumer directed health plans grew in popularity among health benefit managers, and health policy pundits at a time of rising conservatism in the country and in health policy generally.

Third, neither the anticipated growth in CDHP nor the expected effects of CDHP have met the expectations of their most ardent proponents. While there is considerable growth in high-deductible health plans in both the large and small group market, now accounting for some 20% of insured lives, other account-enabled plans such as health savings accounts (HSAs) and health reimbursement arrangements (HRAs)—the true consumer directed health plans— occupy a much smaller share of the market. Equally, CDHP plans are not without their side effects. Drawing extensively on in-depth research conducted by colleagues at Harris Interactive, Kim Slocum analyzes consumers' and employers' experience of consumer directed health plans, in terms of satisfaction with benefits, compliance with medication use, and other important measures of health and patient satisfaction. The picture is not always rosy.

This work sheds fresh light and new insight on an important and growing dimension of American health care. Too much of the literature on CDHP has been either breathless boosterism or unashamed marketing, so it is extremely refreshing to have a work that takes a balanced 360 degree view of consumer directed health care. This book guides us through where they came from, how these plans are working, and where they are headed. It provides insight, analysis, and original research to help us see more clearly this important dimension in the future of health care.

Ian Morrison, PhD
Health Care Futurist
Menlo Park, California

Preface

It is almost impossible to read or watch the news without being bombarded with stories on the problems of the U.S. health care system. You have probably heard at least some of the conflicting proposals about how to fix what is wrong. If you have picked up this book because you are interested in one of the newest trends being touted as the latest "magic bullet" to address our ongoing health care crisis, you have a right to know who is going to tell the story and what you will find between the covers. I have worked in health care essentially all of my adult life. Most of that time was spent as an employee of several pharmaceutical and biotechnology companies. Hopefully, you will not assume I have two horns and a tail (I do not), or that I intend to be an apologist for industry (I will not). For the past fifteen years, I have been involved with health care policy, strategy, and financing issues at a systems level. However, my earlier experiences in the pharmaceutical industry have given me a good perspective on how health care delivery works for those people who are actually in the trenches. One of the things I have learned from all those experiences is that there is not any "they" in health care; there is only "us." For better or worse, we are all in this together. What I have also learned is that politics and ideology have crept into the national debate on health care, and our national discourse is poorer for it. As a result, my perspective is that of a centrist who just wants to see a sustainable health care system in the United States.

I am a strategy person who is interested in the long term. I intend to be a "voyeuristic eunuch" (to take a phrase from my friend Humphrey Taylor). I am very interested in what is happening in health care, and I will try to bring a strategist's viewpoint to the discussion. However, I am not so excited by what I see that I have an ideological "fix" to sell you. What I intend to do is to talk about U.S. health care as dispassionately as I can, to tell you what we know, and to separate that from what one or the other of our ideologies might think. I will distinguish between data collected by people who share my dispassionate approach and that collected by those who have a vested interest in a certain answer to various questions. These are the folks who may be voyeurs but definitely are not eunuchs. Unfortunately, in health care today there are a lot more of the latter than the former. If you are a health policy junkie like me and you are wondering why I did not include your favorite piece of research, that is quite likely to be a reason why. In some cases, I will tell you that, with respect to consumer directed health care, it is still too early to be able to draw reliable conclusions. More than anything else, I want you to understand that health care is about tradeoffs. I am going to pose some of the very large and important "either/or" questions that we are going to have to face sooner or later in the U.S. health care system so that you can understand the choices we are going to have to face.

You also need to know what this book is *not*. I am not writing an academic work, footnoted to nine digits of precision and drafted in the classic academic style. We have lots of work like that—a great deal of it is referenced in the Recommended Reading chapter at the very end of the book. However, a lot of these publications assume a significant degree of familiarity with health policy or economics and are often pretty tough reading for nonexperts. I am hoping this book will be a lot more approachable for folks with an interest in health care who do not happen to have PhDs in economics. This book has been extremely well researched, and I owe a significant debt of gratitude to a number of very famous people in health care who have done much of the basic research that forms the intellectual foundation of what you will read. What I have tried to do is to string the various academic pearls of wisdom together into a story that will make sense to you, while still standing up to a reasonable amount of scholarly scrutiny.

So how will this book unfold? I will start by talking about what is arguably the biggest issue in U.S. health care today—costs. I will talk about the magnitude of the problem in ways you might not have heard before. I will then move on to talk a bit about how the U.S. health care financing system has developed over the past 60-odd years, because it is hard to know where you are going if you do not know where you have been. In the book's second chapter, I will explore the list of "usual suspects" about why U.S. health care is so expensive, and I will try to debunk a few "urban myths" along the way. When we are done with that, the third chapter of the book will turn to talking about "consumer directed" health care. I will take you through the history of high-deductible health plans and the spending accounts that sometimes accompany them. We will review the arguments, both pro and con, and share with you what reliable evidence we have on their effects. In the fourth chapter of the book I will distinguish between the calls for making health care more patient centered and the growing movement to transfer significant portions of financial risk to individual patients through the vehicle of "high-deductible" health plans. I will discuss what a future "consumer directed" system will require and how it might work in practice. At the end of our journey, you will know how we got here, what "here" looks like, and where we might go next.

Hopefully, the combination of the topic and my approach to it has intrigued you enough to want to read more. If so, sit down and settle in for a true story that has more twists and turns than any thriller you might read. It is also one that is still in progress and that will have a direct effect on how long you will live, how well you will live, and how much you will have to pay to do so.

Before we get started, I need to acknowledge a few people who have been instrumental in my development as a health care "wonk." First of all, I want to thank all my friends and colleagues at Harris Interactive—especially Humphrey Taylor and Katherine Binns. Without access to their proprietary data and their encouragement, this book would not have been possible. Similarly, I would like to thank several other organizations upon whose material I have drawn—especially *Health Affairs*, the Commonwealth Fund, the Henry J. Kaiser Family Foundation, the National Center for Policy Analysis, America's Health Insurance Plans, the World Health Organization, the Organization for Economic Cooperation and Development, the California Health Care Foundation, McKinsey & Company, the RAND Corporation, and the Center for Studying Health System Change. All of these organizations granted me permission to cite their data, and I am deeply appreciative. Second, I want to offer a big thanks to my friend Ian Morrison who has been both my role model and my inspiration. I have tried to copy his conversational writing style in the interest of making a lot of the policy issues we will need to discuss a lot more readable. Next, I want to thank a former colleague at AstraZeneca, Deni Deasy Boekell, who was my intellectual partner and sounding board as we labored mightily to create the situation in which we could really think strategically. Finally, I would like to thank my good friend Roger Green, who has consistently encouraged me to explore new frontiers and is a big part of the reason this book exists.

OK, let's get started.

Kim D. Slocum
West Chester, Pennsylvania

Chapter 1

"Baby How'd We Ever Get This Way"

If you are old enough to remember the title of this "golden oldie" from the 1960s, you are also probably old enough to be staring retirement and its attendant medical costs straight in the eye. In fact, if you are an average American over the age of 40 or so, you are likely to be facing a future liability just for medical costs that is bigger than your entire net worth. If this comes as a surprise to you, you are not alone.

Many members of the baby boom generation are now starting to leave the workforce without a particularly clear idea of just how much of a dent out-of-pocket medical spending is likely to make in their nest egg. A recent Harris Interactive survey conducted for the company's Strategic Health Perspectives service found that the overwhelming majority of boomers thought that they would need to spend less than $100,000, and in most cases far less than that amount, on medical care between ages 65 and 80. Work conducted separately by Fidelity Investments and the Employee Benefits Research Institute (EBRI) suggests that the actual number for a couple retiring today at age 65 is somewhere between $250,000 and $550,000. When confronted with these estimates, 73% of boomers in the Harris survey said they were "not at all confident" that they could come up with that much money. If you are planning to live beyond age 80, the numbers continue to escalate from there. Many financial planners now suggest you budget for living to age 90, or even 100, just to be safe. If you do so, and factor health care into the mix, the amount of money you might require to pay for out-of-pocket medical costs over that period of time can easily exceed $1,000,000. When you consider that EBRI has also estimated that a baby boomer's median net worth is somewhere in the range of $100,000, you can easily see the magnitude of the potential funding gap.

It is not just individual consumers who have a problem; this is a potential crisis for the U.S. government as well. A number of federal officials have been sounding alarm bells. In January 2007, Federal Reserve Chairman Ben Bernanke gave testimony before Congress on the financial gap the United States would be facing in its entitlement programs (Social Security, Medicare, and Medicaid) over the next half century. In June 2007, Peter Orszag, head of the Congressional Budget Office (CBO) gave testimony that, if health care costs continued to increase at the same average rate seen over the last several decades, by 2050 spending by the Centers for Medicare & Medicaid Services (CMS) would amount to roughly 20% of the gross domestic product (GDP) of the United States. That is about the size of the entire federal government today. In July 2007, CBO followed up this testimony with a report to Senator Judd Gregg that serves as a reality check on just how big this gap is. According to Director Orszag's report, if health care spending follows its historical pattern and taxation is the only vehicle used to close the funding gap, the highest marginal tax rate in the United States will need to jump from 35% to 92%. If we succeed in cutting the growth in health care spending to 1% more than GDP growth, something many in the health care policy community would regard as a major success, the effect on tax rates could still be profound. The CBO report suggests that, if taxes are the only tool used to close the funding gap in this scenario, the top marginal rate would still need to climb from 35% to 60%.

If you are years away from retirement, perhaps just starting out in the workforce, you may be thinking that this is not really your problem. You are wrong. Apart from the potential tax implications of the problems CMS faces, the ripple effects of the health care cost monster extend even further.

Employers provide health insurance coverage for roughly 150 million Americans, according to the Henry J. Kaiser Family Foundation. A July 2007 analysis conducted by the California HealthCare Foundation showed that, between 1995 and 2005, employer costs for health benefit expenses had grown by 97% versus less than 40% for all other forms of compensation—a more than twofold difference. This same analysis detailed the growth on a per-worker basis and found that premium costs had escalated from $2,056 in 1995 to $3,703 in 2005. In contrast, over that same period, the general rate of inflation ran at about 2% to 3% annually. That represents the amount that most businesses were able to recoup in the form of price increases passed on to their customers. When health care costs grow a rate two to three times higher than price increases, employers are faced with a "grow-in" problem. In other words, the escalating proportion of costs that are consumed by health care means that either business profit shrinks or cutbacks must occur somewhere else. Generally speaking, employees wind up paying more—sometimes a lot more—or losing their health insurance coverage completely.

Do you have a 401(k) plan? Are you invested in stocks or mutual funds? Guess what, the health care cost crisis can hit you there as well. In 2003, the major consulting firm McKinsey & Company conducted an analysis showing that health care benefit costs for employers were equal to about 80% of post-tax corporate profits. They further projected that by 2008, under two different scenarios for profit growth, health care costs would at least equal, if not surpass, corporate profits. In a speech given at the 2007 World Health Care Congress, Steven Burd, CEO of Safeway, said that his firm's health benefit expenses were equal to 105% of the company's profits in 2005. To put these numbers into perspective, financial experts generally believe that the price of a company's stock is made up of two components. The first is the company's earnings—how much profit it makes. The second is the "multiple," which is the number of dollars an investor is prepared to pay today to purchase a dollar of a company's earnings. This number varies a good deal, but for the country's largest firms, represented by the Standard and Poor's 500 Index, it is about 16 to 17. In other words, if the CEOs of American corporations could somehow wave a magic wand and make their health benefit expenses vanish, they could probably double their share price. Think about effectively doubling the value of any stock investments you might own, and you will see how you are affected.

Are you facing copayments or deductibles when you go to your doctor or get a prescription? If so, you have plenty of company, because most people do.

The cost of health care is a reality not just for large governmental agencies and corporations, but for individual consumers as well. The Henry J. Kaiser Family Foundation projects that since 2002 health insurance costs have gone up at a rate roughly four times that of workers' wages. According to data from CMS and the U.S. Census Bureau, while the overall *percentage* of health care paid out of pocket by Americans has not increased much, the absolute *amount* of this expense has. In 1996 the average American household spent $1,841 on health care. By 2005, this had risen by over 44% to $2,664. This was actually a bit smaller than the increase in household income for the same period, so it appears to suggest Americans are paying less in real dollars out of pocket than they were in 1996. However, appearances can be deceiving. The Census Bureau further states that health care costs as a proportion of *all* household spending actually increased from 5.2% to 5.7% over that time. A recent analysis conducted by the Kaiser Family Foundation showed that the proportion of U.S. households facing out-of-pocket health care costs representing 10% or more of their income climbed from 16% to 19% between 1996 and 2003. This effect was seen pretty much across the board at all levels of income. Another February 2006 study by

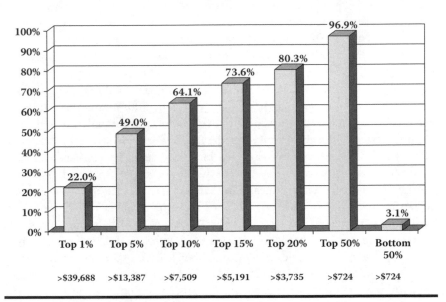

Concentration of U.S. Health Care Spending

Figure 1.1 *Source*: Henry J. Kaiser Family Foundation[1], AHRQ, CMS, and Medicare Expenditure Panel Survey (2004)

the Commonwealth Fund stated that in 2001 through 2002 thirteen million U.S. families had direct out-of-pocket costs equal to or greater than 10% of household income.

If a lot of what you have read so far does not seem to connect with your day-to-day reality, that may be because health care spending is not uniformly distributed. If you draw the short straw economically, you will get a crash course in health care economics, but in any given year, that is a low-probability event. Many of you are probably familiar with the "80/20" rule that says 80% of the effects are due to 20% of the causes (more formally known as the Pareto phenomenon). This certainly works for health care. According to an article published in the January/February 2007 issue of *Health Affairs*, 1% of the U.S. population accounts for more than a quarter of all health care spending, and the top 5% of population accounts for over half of all health care spending. The bottom half of the population spends close to nothing on health care. Figure 1.1 shows just how asymmetrical health care spending actually is.

Health status tends to be correlated with age. The older you are, the more likely you are to require health care. If you live long enough, it is very likely that you will encounter an expensive health problem. Figure 1.2 uses data from the Henry J. Kaiser Family Foundation and CMS to show how this distribution works.

U.S. Health Care Spending by Age

Age In Years	Ave. Spending Per Person
<5	$1,245
5-17	$1,108
18-24	$1,282
25-44	$2,277
45-64	$4,647
>64	$8,647

Figure 1.2 *Source*: **Henry J. Kaiser Family Foundation[2] and CMS**

Health care spending is also related to income and education. The younger and better off you are economically, the better your health status and the less you tend to spend on health care. An October 2006 Henry J. Kaiser Family Foundation poll found that 25% of respondents said they had encountered problems with paying medical bills, and this was a far more common challenge for individuals earning $35,000 a year or less than for those earning more than that amount. So while out-of-pocket health care costs are not a concern for all U.S. residents, they do worry an increasing proportion of the population, especially those at lower income levels.

Every January, CMS releases its updated statistics on health care spending in the United States. This is considered to be the definitive measure of what it costs to take care of the nation's residents. It is lagged by one year (i.e., the January 2007 release told us what happened in 2005, not 2006), but that does not make the information any less compelling. In the thirty-five years from 1970 to 2005, health care spending in the United States grew from $74 billion to $1,987.7 trillion. While the rate of change from 2004 to 2005 was only 6.9%, the third consecutive year of slower growth, this is still about twice the rate of inflation for the entire U.S. economy. Over the past several decades, health care spending has grown at an average of about 10% per year, roughly 2.5% faster than the GDP. This means that, as health care spending has grown, it has become the single largest sector of the U.S. economy, now representing about 16% of everything that we do as a nation. Although CMS is expecting the growth rate to stay below its historical 10% average for the next decade, this still means that health care could represent 20% of the entire economic output of the United States by 2015. It is not necessarily "good" or "bad" that the United States spends that much on health care, but it does represent an opportunity cost. Money invested in health care cannot be spent on other things.

This is not a uniquely American problem. In nearly the entire developed world (usually defined as the United States, Canada, Western Europe, and Japan) health care costs have been increasing as a proportion of GDP. The United States is the world's heavyweight champion of health care spending, though. The Office of Economic Cooperation and Development (OECD) tracks various aspects of the thirty most developed nations on earth, including health care. According to OECD's most recent report, our closest competitors in the health care spending race are France and Switzerland, both of which invested 11% to 12% of GDP in health care in 2005. On a per capita basis, the OECD shows the United States spending $6,401 versus the $4,364 per person spent in Norway, our nearest competitor. According to the World Health Organization (WHO) in 2004, all the countries of the world invested roughly $4.1 trillion in health care for their respective populations. In that same year, CMS reported that the United States spent just under $1.9 trillion on health care. In other words, *46% of the world's total spending in health care occurred in the United States, a nation which accounts for less than 5% of the world's population.*

Health care spending is, of course, only part of the puzzle. The goal of investment in health care is health. Does the United States get better performance, longer life expectancy, healthier citizens, or more quality for its significantly greater investment? This is a much harder question to answer, since it involves a number of subjective measures. However, in general it appears that the United States is not getting a great deal of extra value for its extra spending. The WHO produces ratings on various aspects of health and health care for all nations. It reports that the United States has 2.56 physicians for every 1,000 people. That contrasts with 3.61 in Switzerland or 3.37 in both France and Germany. The United States has more physicians per 1,000 than Canada (2.14), Japan (1.98), or the United Kingdom (2.30), but not as many more as might be expected given the vast disparity in per capita health care spending.

Looking at life expectancy, a similar pattern emerges. An American male can expect to live 75 years, with an American female living five years longer to age 80. In Canada, those numbers are 78 and 83, respectively. For the United Kingdom, they are 77 and 81. In France, 77 and 84. For Germany, 76 and 82. For Japan, life expectancy is 79 years for men and 86 years for women. All our additional spending does not seem to buy us longer lives. Figure 1.3 represents a summary of the comparisons derived from the WHO.

In 1999, the Institute of Medicine issued its now-famous report *To Err Is Human*, in which it suggested that the health care delivery system killed between 48,000 and 98,000 Americans annually due to preventable medical

Selected Statistics on Health Care Systems

COUNTRY	Health Care $ Per Capita	% GDP Devoted to Health Care	MDs/ 1,000	RNs/ 1,000	Hospital Beds/ 1,000	Male Life Expectancy	Female Life Expectancy	Cardiovascular Mortality Rate	Cancer Mortality Rate
Canada	$3,038	9.8%	2.14	9.95	36	78	83	141	138
France	$3,464	10.5%	3.37	7.24	75	77	84	162	148
Germany	$3,521	10.6%	3.37	9.72	84	76	82	141	84
Italy	$2,580	8.7%	4.20	5.44	40	78	84	174	134
Japan	$2,823	7.8%	1.98	7.79	129	79	86	106	119
Switzerland	$5,572	11.5%	0.16	4.24	57	79	84	142	116
United Kingdom	$2,900	8.1%	2.30	12.12	39	77	81	182	143
United States	$6,096	15.4%	2.56	9.37	33	75	80	188	134

Figure 1.3 *Source*: **Data from the World Health Organization**

errors. Subsequent reports have suggested that number may be too low. The U.S. Census Bureau reports that, in 2005, 44.8 million Americans—15.3% of our population—had no health insurance coverage at all and therefore no easy way to access the care delivery system.

The bottom line is simply this. The United States spends an enormous amount on health care, and when compared to other nations in the developed world, it does not seem to get more infrastructure or more life expectancy for its investment. Our spending does not provide health insurance coverage for our entire population, and the delivery system itself can be dangerous. While these are certainly not the only indicators of quality one could apply, they do suggest that Americans are not getting outputs from their health care system proportional to the costs incurred.

Do I have your attention? While lots of problems occupy our day-to-day consciousness, they often come and go pretty quickly. Health care problems have been going on for decades and affect everyone somehow.

If health care spending is a problem for all three of the potential payer audiences, it is logical to ask how we ever got into this position. There is no shortage of theories to explain this unhappy situation, and we will explore several of the leading contenders. Before we turn to a discussion of the various hypotheses and show how much or little support there is for each, it is helpful to take a short side trip to talk about health insurance and how it works. Since those who are the staunchest advocates of consumer directed health care often point to third-party payment as one of the major culprits behind U.S. health care cost escalation, it is important to understand a bit of the background of how it came to be.

It is not entirely certain when health insurance started in the United States. Some reports suggest that it had its origins in the accident insurance first issued in the United States during the Civil War (1861–1865). These policies only covered mishaps incurred in rail or steamboat travel, so they may not qualify as "health insurance." The first true illness and disability policies were offered around 1890. However, before the 1920s, the state of medical technology was still relatively primitive, and hospitals were places to be avoided if at all possible. As a result, most patients received rather low-tech treatments in their own homes. Health care was relatively inexpensive, and the most economically challenging part of illness was the loss of income suffered if one was too sick to work.

Throughout the early years of the twentieth century, advances in medical technology began to accumulate. X-rays were discovered in 1895, and several years afterward the first crude radiologic imaging equipment became available. Aseptic technique became more common, thereby reducing the hospital infection rate. The very first antibiotics were developed during the 1930s, which meant that an infection was no longer such a frequent death sentence. The result of this was that medical care started to become both more beneficial and more expensive.

In 1929, a group of teachers in Dallas, Texas, started the first prepaid group insurance program when they set up an agreement with Baylor Hospital to provide medical services in exchange for a monthly fee. In 1932, the first nonprofit Blue Cross and Blue Shield plans were formed as an extension of the efforts of those Dallas teachers. These plans offered physicians and hospitals more volume in exchange for reduced fees.

Throughout the late nineteenth century national health care insurance became part of the landscape in parts of Europe as well. For example, in 1883, the Workers' Health Insurance Act came into effect in Prussia, and over the next two decades much of the infrastructure needed to deliver health care to the population of an entire country was assembled. In France, the "mutuelles" (health insurance plans) covered many citizens during the late 1800s before the beginning of the country's "Assurance Sociales," a statutory means-tested program that began in 1930.

In the United States, though, health insurance remained relatively uncommon, and attempts to create some sort of national coverage system failed to generate the sort of momentum seen on the other side of the Atlantic. By 1940, only about ten million Americans were enrolled in health insurance plans. However, an event was about to occur that would change this situation and lay the groundwork for the health insurance system that exists in the United States today.

As the story goes, an American industrialist, possibly the magnate Henry J. Kaiser, was sitting in his office in Richmond, California, one day. World War II had recently begun, and he had just won the contract from the U.S. government to build the Liberty Ships that were to be used to ferry cargo across the Atlantic and Pacific oceans. Unfortunately, most of the men he would normally have hired to construct these ships were going into uniform to fight. To make matters worse, President Roosevelt had recently imposed wage and price controls on the country to prevent an outbreak of inflation. The question on Kaiser's mind was how to find the workers he desperately needed to fulfill his contract. He knew that shipbuilding was a dangerous occupation, with a relatively high number of on-the-job injuries. As he looked around, he also saw a workforce that had a higher-than-average propensity to need health care, namely men with physical problems who had been rejected for military service, and women who often had dependent children at home. He came up with the idea of offering health care as a form of noncash compensation to attract the needed workers. Kaiser had already gotten some experience with the idea of employer-funded health care. In 1933 Kaiser's firm, along with several others, had formed an insurance consortium called Industrial Indemnity to assist with meeting workers' compensation obligations. Kaiser asked Sidney Garfield, the physician with whom he had worked a decade earlier, to set something up for workers at the Richmond shipyard. A full package of prepaid health care benefits was a result, and this arrangement later became the major health care provider/insurer Kaiser Permanente.

While all the elements this story may or may not be completely accurate, it is true that the combination of a labor shortage and wage/price controls was a powerful spur for employers across the country to begin offering health insurance as part of a broader compensation package. Health care was among the first "fringe benefits" offered American workers. The Internal Revenue Service (IRS) also provided an important stimulus. In a series of rulings over a number of years, the IRS allowed employers to deduct the cost of providing health insurance for workers as a business expense. This was in contrast to what happened at the individual level where insurance premiums were considered an ordinary expense for tax purposes and, therefore, not tax deductible. Since tax rates in the United States during the 1950s were far higher than those seen today, this differential advantage for employers was very significant. As a result, as shown in Figure 1.4, health insurance enrollment in the United States skyrocketed between 1940 and 1960, largely driven by the role of employers.

1974 saw another major milestone in employer-sponsored health insurance. During that year, Congress passed the Employee Retirement Income Security Act (ERISA). While ERISA was primarily intended to tighten regulation of

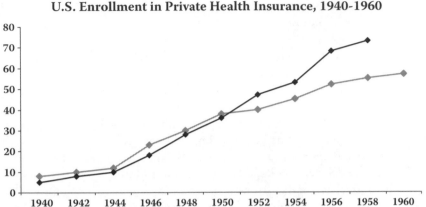

U.S. Enrollment in Private Health Insurance, 1940-1960

Figure 1.4 *Source*: Blumenthal D.N Engl J Med 2006; 335:82–88

pension plans, it also affected other sorts of employee benefit plans including health insurance, if such plans met certain requirements. In particular two of its provisions were of critical importance for employer-sponsored health insurance. First, ERISA formalized the various IRS rulings about the tax deductibility of employers' health insurance expenses. Second, it created the "ERISA preemption." In brief, this stated that "self-insured" employer benefit plans (meaning those employers who did not pass the financial risk of such plans on to other entities like insurance companies) that operated across state lines were exempt from the laws of the individual states and instead were to be held accountable to the standards described in ERISA. This made employers accountable primarily to the U.S. Department of Labor, rather than other sorts of regulators and licensors who control the rest of health care, primarily at the state level.

Given all these advantages, it is hardly surprising that enrollment in employer-sponsored health insurance continued to escalate. In 2000, about 69% of all employers offered health insurance to employees, as well as some dependents and retirees. While, largely due to the escalating costs discussed earlier, the percentage of employers offering health care insurance has recently fallen to 61%, over 150 million Americans obtain their health insurance coverage through employers.

The other major pieces of the U.S. health insurance puzzle are the programs that cover poor, elderly, and disabled Americans. President Harry Truman had requested a national health insurance plan in 1945, and there was some consideration given to national health insurance during the Roosevelt administration. However, the federal government's role in health care largely dates back to enactment of the Social Security Act Amendments of 1965, which established the Medicare and Medicaid programs. These were part of President Lyndon Johnson's "Great Society" initiatives and represented the first substantive government-funded program to provide health care for a significant portion of the nonmilitary, nonveteran, nongovernment-employee segment of the U.S. population. These amendments were controversial at the time and became law over the strenuous objections of organized medicine, which decried them as a trend toward "socialized medicine." Interestingly, former President Harry Truman was the nation's first Medicare enrollee. Within three years of its enactment, he had been joined by twenty million additional senior citizens.

Before the Medicare program, elderly Americans were expected to pay for health care out of their own pockets, or through some form of private insurance. As a result, it was very possible for a single catastrophic illness to drain the life savings of a retiree, thereby impoverishing them at a time when they could no longer work to replenish the money that had been spent. While Medicare was (and still is) far from full insurance against medical costs, it did shore up the economic security of older Americans by insulating them to some extent from the costs of hospital and physician services. In addition to the elderly, starting in 1972 Medicare was extended to cover permanently disabled Americans under the age of 65 and those with end-stage renal disease. In successive years, coverage for hospice care, chiropractic care, physical therapy, and speech therapy were added. In the late 1980s coverage for routine mammograms and pap smears was added. The largest recent expansion of the program came in December 2003 with the passage of the Medicare Modernization Act, which provided the first routine coverage of outpatient prescription drugs and also reestablished the opportunity for private insurance companies to participate in Medicare. According to the Henry J. Kaiser Family Foundation, slightly more than forty-four million Americans are enrolled in the Medicare program today.

The Medicaid program was also established as part of the 1965 legislation, and it did a number of things. First, it helped low-income elderly Americans with the out-of-pocket costs required for participation in the Medicare program. It also provided medical care for some low-income nonelderly Americans, the blind, the disabled, and those with dependent children. Contrary to popular opinion, Medicaid does not cover all indigent Americans, but only those who fit into certain defined categories. Medicaid is jointly funded by the federal government and the states. The proportions coming from each of these sources vary from state to state, but across the entire country, the federal government provides about 57% of all Medicaid funding. In 2004, roughly 57.5 million Americans were enrolled in Medicaid, including about 6 million who qualify for both the Medicare and Medicaid programs (the "dual eligibles").

Health Care Financing in Selected Countries

COUNTRY	% Paid By Government	% Paid By Private Sources	% Paid By Third Parties (Government+ Private Insurance)	% Paid Out-Of-Pocket
Canada	69.8%	30.2%	85.1%	14.9%
France	78.4%	21.6%	92.5%	7.5%
Germany	76.9%	23.1%	86.7%	13.3%
Italy	75.1%	24.9%	79.0%	21.0%
Japan	81.3%	18.7%	82.3%	17.7%
Switzerland	58.5%	41.5%	68.2%	31.8%
UK	86.3%	13.7%	87.4%	12.6%
US	44.7%	55.3%	86.9%	13.1%

Figure 1.5 *Source*: **Data from the World Health Organization**

According to CMS, the total spending for Medicare in 2005 was about $342 billion, while the total spending for Medicaid (federal and state funds combined) was about $319 billion. These two programs alone account for over one-third of all health care spending in the United States, and CMS is the largest single entity paying for health care in the entire country.

While the U.S. market has its own particular blend of public and private-sector financing, what is not unusual is the role of third-party payment for health care. As Figure 1.5 (derived from WHO data) shows, throughout most of the developed world, third-party payment, either through government agencies or through private insurance is the standard procedure by which health care is financed.

Economists are quick to point out that, in reality, consumers/patients actually wind up paying for all health care; the real question is the mechanism by which that occurs. Health care can be financed out of pocket by the individual who needs it at the time of service. It can also be financed through taxation. Finally, it can be paid for in the form of withheld wages such as we see in the employer-sponsored segment of the U.S. health care insurance market. Each of these has very different ramifications for individuals and society as a whole. However, the degree to which the developed world has settled on the concept of indirect/third-party payment is remarkable.

Why is third-party payment so common? There are two primary reasons. The first goes back to the most basic principle of insurance. Many individuals pay a small amount in premiums each year so that a few people who experience a loss can receive compensation. The technical term for this is "risk pooling," and it is especially important in health insurance. As we have already seen, health care expenses are not evenly divided among a population. If there is not some means of spreading the economic risk of illness, then becoming sick would be a ticket to financial ruin for almost everyone but the very wealthiest. The second important reason third-party payment is so common is that it allows individuals who will be receiving health care to be aggregated into a large buying pool. This permits them to negotiate with health care providers for better prices. Whether such buying pools are created by government agencies or private insurance companies, they are an important tool in helping to contain health care costs.

Under certain circumstances, it is possible in the United States to purchase individual insurance coverage, but because of factors relating to expense and risk pooling, this represents only a very small fraction of the population. Such insurance may be purchased for a brief time to bridge coverage when individuals are between jobs, or it can be purchased for longer periods of time, such as by those who are self-employed. Reliable estimates of exactly how many Americans are covered by individual insurance are difficult to come by, but a 2004 projection from the Center for Studying Health System Change put the number at a maximum of 5.5% of the nonelderly U.S. population. A 2004 paper published in the journal *Health Affairs* suggested that about half of those covered by "nongroup" policies were self-employed, while the balance seemed to be "bridging" coverage gaps between insurance obtained from employers. This nongroup insurance market is notoriously unstable, and coverage can be extremely difficult to obtain at reasonable prices. Individuals suffering from even relatively minor health care problems may be uninsurable in the nongroup market at any price.

Because individual insurance can be difficult to obtain and expensive, the bulk of Americans who do not fall into one of various purchasing groups generally wind up uninsured. According to a March 2007 press release from the U.S. Census Bureau, 44.8 million Americans, or about 15.3% of the population were without health insurance of any kind. The health policy community devotes a good deal of effort to studying precisely who is uninsured in United States, and this is a topic of considerable debate even among experts. In 2005, eight in ten of the uninsured came from working families, almost 70% from families with one or more full-time workers. Adults are also more likely to be uninsured than children. Roughly 80% of the uninsured are native or naturalized U.S. citizens, and 59% have been without coverage for at least two years. Interestingly, while the lack of health insurance is traditionally thought of as a problem facing the poor, a rising number of the uninsured come from middle-class households, defined as those with incomes between $40,000 and $59,900.

Insurance coverage matters, because it has a large bearing on health status, and because lack of insurance has economic consequences for society as a whole. Studies have shown that individuals without health care insurance have decreased access to care, receive less preventative care, are less likely to fill prescriptions they receive for medications, and as a result are more likely to be hospitalized for avoidable problems. Patients without insurance also have worse health outcomes. Under federal law, no patient can be denied care in an emergency room because he or she lacks the ability to pay for it. As a result, the emergency room is a common place where the health problems of the uninsured get managed. In fact, the uninsured are twice as likely as those with insurance to visit emergency rooms or to be hospitalized. However, emergency rooms are only required to stabilize patients, and this is a far cry from the more comprehensive care often required by such patients to treat the root causes of their problems. Finally, emergency rooms and inpatient hospital beds are some of the most expensive sites for health care delivery in the United States.

A high proportion of the costs for care the uninsured do receive are often borne by the remainder of the population in the form of higher premiums, thereby making it an issue of economic as well as humanitarian concern. Since most of the uninsured are under the age of 65, negative health outcomes such individuals encounter also have broader effects, since they impact their potential productivity as employees. One expert suggested that the total economic burden of uninsurance in the United States is in the range of $65 billion to $130 billion annually. A second survey conducted by Families USA found that, in 2005, premium costs for family health insurance coverage provided by private employers included an extra $922 in premiums due to the cost of care for the uninsured; premiums for individual coverage included an extra $341.

The United States is obviously not the only country on Earth. How is health care delivery structured and financed in other parts of the developed world? As shown in Figure 1.5, governmental agencies generally play a larger role in health care finance in most of Europe and in Japan—in most cases a much larger role. This does not imply that either our U.S. system or systems found abroad are inherently superior or inferior. What it does mean is that they are different.

In his article entitled "Why Is a Systemic View of Health Care Financing Necessary?" in the July/August 2007 issue of *Health Affairs*, Harvard's William Hsiao discussed the ways in which health care can be organized and the strategic-level plusses and minuses of each. He cited previous work from Brian Abel-Smith describing "direct" and "indirect" provision of health care. In the direct model, a government agency, usually a ministry of health, will receive a budget from a country's treasury function, then allocate these funds among doctors and hospitals who are employees of the Health Ministry. This is true "government-controlled health care." The indirect model is quite different. It involves a split between the funding of health care, which still has a strong government footprint, and the actual delivery of care, which is accomplished by privately employed doctors and hospitals. The indirect model can be further subdivided into two categories, depending on whether a government agency (the "public trust" model) or private entities (the "surrogate" model) make the decisions about where health care dollars will be invested. While the direct model is popular in less-developed countries, most of the nations that could generally be considered to be peers of the United States use some form of the indirect model. In other words, true socialized medicine is uncommon in the developed world.

In countries such as France, Germany, and Japan, individual citizens are usually required to join "sickness funds," which are quasi-public bodies that provide funding and risk pooling for health insurance. Coverage obtained from a sickness fund is portable—it is not tied to employment. Contrary to the beliefs of many people, patients can select their physicians. Some degree of patient payment at the time of service is required, although these systems are predominately funded through a blend of taxation and insurance premiums.

In the United Kingdom, Italy, and Canada, health care is administered through governmental agencies. It is important to note that, in Canada, most care is provided by private doctors and hospitals. While the government funds most physician and hospital services, prescription drugs, dental care, and other services are funded either out of pocket or through private insurance. In the United Kingdom, medical services are funded through taxation and delivered by private physicians who contract with the National Health Service. Payment at the point of service is not required, leading some to mistakenly refer to the care as "free." Since tax rates are considerably higher in the United Kingdom than in the United States, it is more correct to say that health care services are "prepaid." Patients also have the opportunity to select their physician in these countries. Individuals can purchase private insurance to avoid having to wait to receive services. The Italian health care system operates in a fashion similar to that of the United Kingdom.

There are fundamental cultural differences between Europe, Japan, and the United States. In most of the rest of developed world, universal insurance coverage is the rule. However, this coverage is generally subsidized, and there are large risk pools. Part of the difference between the U.S. system and those found elsewhere can be explained by the fact that there is far more social solidarity abroad than in the United States, a belief that "we're all in this together." As a result, health care in these countries is considered a right rather than a market good. However, the tax rates required to support such health care systems are significantly higher than those paid by Americans, and in some cases there are considerable waits required for patients to receive at least some forms of care. In short, these nations have made different tradeoffs between some aspects of health care (e.g., universal access) and other societal priorities (e.g., tax rates). There are no "magic bullets," but there may be selected lessons that Americans can learn by studying how health care systems are organized and financed in other parts of the world.

Enoch Powell was minister of health for the United Kingdom's National Health Service back in the early 1960s. He is reported to have said "there is virtually no upper limit to the amount of health care an individual can consume." This one statement summarizes the problem faced by all nations and cultures everywhere. Health care is something that people want in ever-increasing quantities. Humphrey Taylor of Harris Interactive refers to it as a "superior good." By that he means that, as a country's gross domestic product increases and extra resources become available, health care is one of the two leading places where citizens want to see more funds allocated (education is the other). This is not particularly surprising if you think about it. Generally speaking, people are genetically "hard wired" to want to live the longest, healthiest lives they possibly can, and they also want to provide the best opportunities possible for their children. With respect to health care, though, this creates a problem. No society can afford to devote unlimited resources to health care. In the most basic economic terms, the demand for health care always exceeds its supply. As a result, all societies need to make decisions about how to allocate the relatively scarce resources available for health care to the members of that society who wish to receive them. In other words, health care has to be rationed.

"Rationing" is often considered to be a dirty word in health care, especially in the United States. A common complaint about health care systems seen in other countries is that they ration health care—and this is something few Americans would voluntarily accept. However, the United States faces the same problems as every other nation in terms of demand and supply, so it also needs to address the allocation question, it needs to ration care. In fact, *every health care system in the world, including the United States, has always rationed care.* The key question is how that care is rationed.

Economists say that any scarce resource can be rationed on the supply side or on the demand side. In health care, that roughly translates to "what sort of care is available?" (supply side), and "how much does it cost a patient to access it?" (demand side). In most of the rest of the developed world, rationing is accomplished primarily by limiting the supply of health care. Given the general tilt toward greater public funding of health care abroad, this is not particularly surprising. There are finite numbers of hospitals and physicians available to treat patients. New technologies are subject to rigorous cost-effective analysis before they can be sold. As a result, people in these countries often have to wait to receive at least some forms of medical care. This problem can become quite challenging for nonemergency elective care such as hip replacements. If a country does not allocate sufficient resources to the supply of health care, the "wait list" problem can spill over into treatment of more serious conditions as well.

The other way to ration care is through its price, and this is primarily how it is done in the United States. If a patient wishes to receive care but is unable to afford it, it generally does not get delivered (with the exception of true medical emergencies discussed above). This economic reality check serves essentially the same function as the waiting lists that are used abroad. It limits the amount of care that actually gets delivered, thereby limiting how much of society's scarce resources are to be devoted to health care spending.

So which way of rationing health care is "better"? There is an old saying that goes "where you stand depends on where you sit," and that is particularly true for this very difficult question. Neither of these means of rationing care is inherently superior to the other; they just create problems for different groups of people.

If you live in a country that rations health care by limiting its supply, but at the same time makes the care that is provided available to you at limited out-of-pocket cost, that is likely to be more appealing to you if you are relatively poorer. If, on the other hand, you are better off economically, you are likely to resent the fact that there is technology that might improve your health but is not available to you in your home country. Since these countries tend to have higher tax rates, this can be a double whammy. You pay more in taxes than if you lived in a society that rationed care differently, but you still cannot always get all the health care you might like. If you are rich enough, you are likely to try to find some other way of using your money to get access to it.

This accounts for the stories we sometimes see in the U.S. press about wealthy foreigners who come to the United States to receive high-end medical treatment for various medical conditions. It also accounts, in large part, for the spread of private insurance plans in nations like the United Kingdom. Well-off individuals can use their assets to "jump the queue" by purchasing insurance plans that offer them instant access to medical technology they might otherwise have to wait in line to receive. Being relatively poorer is much less of an obstacle to care in such systems. You pay a higher rate of taxes than in "demand-rationing" countries, but since your income is lower, so are your taxes. You get to receive at least some level of care at little or no out-of-pocket cost, largely because a lot of care is cross-subsidized by the higher taxes paid by your better-off fellow citizens.

If you live in a country that rations on the demand side of health care, everything is reversed. Since there are fewer barriers to making care available, there tends to be essentially anything you want—but at a price. Being well off in a society that rations health care on the demand side can be a bit like visiting

Disneyland. Lots of shiny new medical toys can be had, and you have the means to afford them. Your tax rates are lower, so you can keep more of your assets, and you are able to spend them as you see fit. If you are unfortunate enough to be on the other end of the economic spectrum in such a country, access to health care can look like a mirage. You can see it all around you, but you cannot get at it yourself, because you cannot afford it.

Depending on precisely how expensive care actually is, there may be a few people affected by this problem, or it can become a major issue for a large segment of the population. These societies tend to have far higher numbers of people without health insurance, and the big discussion tends to revolve around the fairness of having some number of people deprived of health care access. Such countries need to have "safety valve" programs to address the worst access inequality problems, or their societies can become unstable. This helps to explain why programs like Medicare and Medicaid exist in the United States. Even though Americans feel a great deal of angst about health care costs, the pressures would be much worse if these programs did not exist.

In the end, the choice comes down to whether health care is a market good or a societal right. That is the most fundamental question, and it affects how you feel about the way health care resources should be rationed. If you think that health care is not different in any fundamental way from any other product or service and that free markets are the best way to allocate resources, then you probably belong to the former group. If you are a proponent of social solidarity and a believer that health is a critical precondition for attainment of other life goals, you are probably in the latter group.

Your economic status is a strong influencer of how you respond to this question. People who are better off are generally more likely to be in the market good camp, in part because they are less likely to have problems purchasing health care. People at the lower end of the economic pyramid are often more likely to support the societal right position, in part because they would otherwise be priced out of the health care market. Much of the problem we face in reaching a shared view on how to address our health care problems comes from the fact that each of these positions has become something of an article of faith with our country's opposite ideological poles, and this can make it very difficult to have an unemotional discussion about where we need to go and what we need to do.

So, as we come to the close of this first chapter, let us tie these various threads together and see what conclusions we can reach. First, we have seen that health care costs are a major challenge for the United States, and the problem is likely to intensify over the next decade or so as the baby boom generation starts to age into Medicare. Simply avoiding the very painful discussion about what to do is not an option. Although the United States spends a good deal more on health care than other nations, it does not seem that we get the sort of "bang for the buck" in terms of life expectancy or medical infrastructure that you might expect. This problem also shows little sign of spontaneously fixing itself.

Looking back at the evolution of health care finance in the United States shows that, as medical science advanced, beginning roughly with the start of the twentieth century, health care began to get too expensive for most people to manage as an out-of-pocket cost. Health insurance evolved to help address this problem. However, health insurance did not become a fixture in the United States until employers made it part of the overall compensation package, and this started due to a series of historical accidents. The federal government has been a significant participant in providing coverage for selected groups of Americans for roughly the past forty years. Third-party payment is very significant, not just in the United States, but everywhere in the developed world. Employers play a unique role in helping to subsidize the U.S. health insurance market, but coverage obtained through employment appears to be on the decline. If you are unfortunate enough not to be a member of a group eligible for health insurance coverage, you are likely to be uninsured and will probably experience worse health outcomes as result. A portion of the costs for the care received by the uninsured becomes part of the expense for health insurance coverage for everyone else.

Other nations that are part of the developed world (Western Europe and Japan) face the same challenges of how to finance health care that America does, but have come up with quite different solutions. These alternatives are not necessarily better or worse than what we see in the United States, but do represent a different series of societal choices.

More than anything else, I would like you to take one key thought from this quick trip through the history of health care insurance. Almost everything to do with health care involves a tradeoff. You can have nearly anything you want, but you may have to give up something else to get it. As a result, there are a lot of "either/or" questions that have to be considered. There are no right or wrong answers to these questions, but rather a series of choices that have to be made. Let us start to frame some of these big questions, and I will ask you to keep them in mind as we move through the rest of our journey.

1. Is health care an individual responsibility, or is it something that we all share?
2. Is health care a societal right, or is it a market good?
3. Would you be willing to trade higher tax rates for universal coverage and access to care?
4. Would you be willing to wait to receive some forms of health care in exchange for paying less to receive it?

Chapter 2

"The Usual Suspects"

There is no shortage of theories about why health care in the United States costs so much more than it does everywhere else in the world. The various hypotheses advanced to explain the situation cover a considerable amount of ideological ground, and the numerous arguments made by the assorted groups of true believers in each could easily fill their own book. However, in this chapter we will discuss eight of the most popular theories and look at the evidence that does (or does not) support them. As you read through this chapter, please bear in mind that, while we will be looking at these factors as if they were completely independent of each other, that is not entirely correct. Health care is extremely complex, and the various factors involved in making it expensive are interrelated to some degree.

Before we begin this exploration, it is helpful to take a look at exactly where the two trillion dollars spent on U.S. health care actually goes. Figure 2.1 is taken from Centers for Medicare & Medicaid Services (CMS) data for 2005 and shows the breakdown of spending by category.

There are a couple of important observations to make from this data. First, the biggest single cost component for health care in the United States is hospital care. This has been true since CMS and its predecessor agencies started keeping track of detailed data more than forty years ago. While there has been some minor year-to-year variation, hospitals have consistently accounted for about a third of U.S. health care spending. Physician services are the second biggest cost category. Once again, the data have been quite consistent across several decades; physician services have accounted for between 20% and 25% of U.S. health care spending. Since these two categories alone represent more than half of our

U.S. Health Care Spending—Where The Money Goes

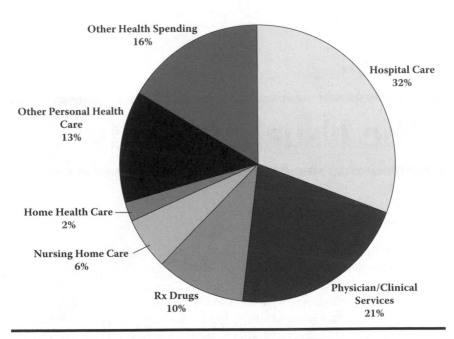

Other Health Spending
16%

Hospital Care
32%

Other Personal Health
Care
13%

Home Health Care —
2%

Nursing Home Care —
6%

Rx Drugs
10%

Physician/Clinical
Services
21%

Figure 2.1 *Source*: **Based on data from OECD Health Data**

total national investment in health care, if we are looking for explanations for why U.S. health care costs so much, at least part of the answer must lie here. Prescription drugs are a distant third and have contributed between 7% and 11% each year for the past four decades. Other types of spending are very small in comparison.

Health care spending looks very different from the point of view of the consumer. Figure 2.2 shows how the roughly $250 billion in out-of-pocket spending is distributed. Prescription drugs are the single largest component of consumer spending, with physician services and dental care trailing. Note that the single biggest component of national spending, hospital care, is only a relatively small fraction of consumer out-of-pocket spending. There is a list of "Murphy's Laws," one of which says "where you stand on an issue depends on where you sit." That is very true for health care where the policy community spends most of its time looking at the overall national picture, while average consumers are more concerned about the very different costs that make up their out-of-pocket spending. It also helps to explain why policy makers and average consumers sometimes

U.S. Out-Of-Pocket Spending On Health Care

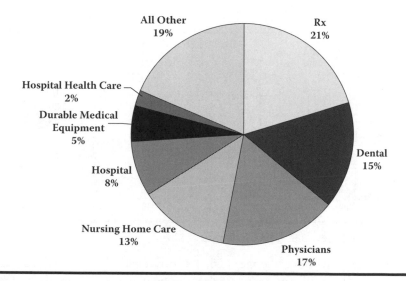

Figure 2.2 *Source*: **Based on data from OECD Health Data**

talk past each other on questions of health care spending. If we are actually going to find some answers to the U.S. health care bill, though, we do need to take the perspective of the policy makers and look at the big picture.

Aging Population?

This is one of the most common theories advanced for the growth in U.S. health care spending, and it gets expressed so often, many people simply assume it must be true. We have already discussed the financial pressure that the Medicare program, driven in part by the baby boom generation, is likely to put on health care finance. Since "Gen X" and other subsequent generations are smaller than the boomer generation, this obviously means that we are growing older as a country.

The Census Bureau not only counts how many people live in the United States, but also makes a number of projections about how the population will look at various points in the future. According to its most recent projections, shown in Figure 2.3, the United States is clearly aging. By 2050, about 21% of

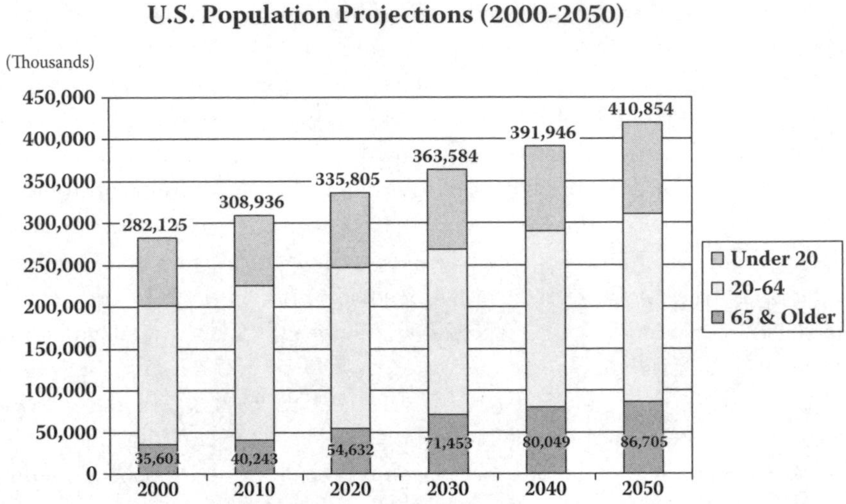

U.S. Population Projections (2000-2050)

(Thousands)

Figure 2.3   *Source*: **U.S. Census Bureau**

our population will be over the age of 65, in contrast with about 12% in that age bracket in 2000. While the country's overall population will grow about 45% over that period, the 65+ segment is projected to grow by over 240%. At the same time, the proportion of our population aged 20 to 64, or what is normally considered working age, will decline from 59% to 53% of the total.

We have already seen the effect aging has on health care spending. It costs roughly three to five times as much to take care of a person over 65 as it does for someone of working age. This must make a huge difference in health care spending, right?

Although it may seem hard to believe, there is less than meets the eye here. Experts have taken a careful look at this question and concluded that the effect of aging per se is fairly minor. In 2003, Dr. Uwe Reinhardt of Princeton published a paper in *Health Affairs* in which he looked at all the studies conducted not just in the United States, but in other countries. His conclusion was "the aging of the population is too gradual a process to rank as a major cost driver for health care."

Let us try to understand why. We are talking about a shift of roughly 9% of the population spread over a period of forty years, and it turns out that is not enough of a change to explain much of the annual change in health costs all by itself. Some fairly simple calculations will show why this is so. Looking at the Census Bureau's projections by decade shows that we are really going to face a twenty-year period where the elderly population will increase a lot on an annual

Percentage of Population 65 Or Older and Life Expectancy

COUNTRY	% Of Population Aged 65 or Older	Life Expectancy For Females at Age 65 (Years)	Life Expectancy For Males at Age 65 (Years)
Canada	12.6%	20.4	16.8
France	16.0%	21.2	16.7
Germany	16.4%	19.4	15.7
Italy	18.1%	20.4	16.5
Japan	17.2%	22.4	17.5
Switzerland	16.0%	20.7	16.9
United Kingdom	15.8%	18.9	15.7
United States	12.3%	19.2	16.3

Figure 2.4 *Source*: **Based on data from OECD Health Data**

basis. From 2010 to 2020 the increase will run at about 3% per year and will drop off a bit to about 2.75% per year from 2020 to 2030. For the rest of the time, the increase in the elderly population will be only about 1% to 1.5% per year. While that is a lot of people in absolute terms, it is a lot less scary when measured against a population that grows from 282 million in 2002 to almost 420 million by 2020.

If we compare the United States with other developed nations, we see that aging alone just does not explain a lot of differences in costs between countries. Using 2000 data from the Office of Economic Cooperation and Development (OECD), shown in Figure 2.4, the United States actually had a *lower* percentage of its population aged 65 or more that year versus other developed nations. We have already seen that these nations all spend a good deal less on health care than does the United States, so an aging population cannot explain the difference in costs between the United States and its counterparts. Skeptics might suggest that these nations limit the effect of aging by restricting the use of health care by older residents. While we do not have a perfect measure to show how other nations operate, we can get a crude metric by measuring life expectancy for elderly residents. Figure 2.4 also shows 2000 OECD data on the years of life expectancy for a 65-year-old in these countries. The United States actually ranks near the bottom of the list for females and is in the middle of the pack for males. While health care certainly is not the only determinant of life expectancy for elderly people, the data do suggest that these other nations at least are not reducing health care spending by shortening the lives of their senior citizens.

There is at least one further bit of evidence to suggest aging may not be the problem for health care costs that many people believe. According to CMS data, the Medicare program has represented a relatively stable proportion of U.S. health care spending over the last quarter century, staying in the range of 15% to 18% throughout that period, and actually declining from 1999 to 2004. While, as we have seen, Medicare is not exclusively devoted to health care for the elderly, and it does not cover all expenses associated with health care for America's senior citizens, it does represent a partial surrogate for this population's health care costs.

There are other factors associated with the aging of the U.S. population that may influence health care costs in other ways. As the proportion of our population in the 20 to 64 age bracket decreases of the next several decades, there will be less workers available for all industries, including health care. This could affect health care more than many other industries, because health care has traditionally been quite labor intensive. For example, more than half the cost of operating a hospital involves paying wages and benefits for workers. Unlike many other industries, health care has not benefited to a great extent from productivity-enhancing tools such as information technology. As a result, health care is still heavily dependent on its workers, and if they become scarcer, this could make health care more expensive.

Malpractice Judgments and Defensive Medicine?

Invariably when the question of why health care in the United States costs so much, the U.S. legal system and malpractice insurance will get at least a mention. How big a drain are malpractice judgments on the U.S. health care system? The answer is surprisingly little. In a 2005 article published in *Health Affairs*, Gerard Anderson and his colleagues looked at the question as part of a broader examination of U.S. health care spending. They compared malpractice judgments in the United States to those in Canada, the United Kingdom, and Australia—all of which share similar legal systems. They concluded that, while the United States had almost 50% more claims filed than the United Kingdom and Australia, two-thirds of these claims did not result in a judgment against the defendant. The average U.S. settlement was actually smaller that those awarded in Canada or the United Kingdom, and the real annual growth in total payments from 1997 to 2001 was smaller than in any of the other three nations. In none of the four nations studied did malpractice judgments account for more than 0.5% of health care spending. They also made an effort to evaluate the effect of "defensive medicine"—doctors ordering more tests than are necessary, but were unable to reach any final conclusions because it was difficult to separate the effect of legal concerns from other pressures on physicians regarding their ordering procedures. However, since the number and size of judgments did not vary dramatically between the four nations, it seems unlikely the there would be any significant differences in defensive medicine between them. As a result, neither malpractice suits, nor defensive medicine seem to be a major contributor to the difference in health care costs between the United States and the rest of the world. This view was reinforced by an analysis conducted by the U.S. Congressional Budget Office which concluded in a 2004 analysis that reducing defensive medicine would have only a small effect on U.S. health care costs.

Malpractice insurance premiums have unquestionably gone up over the past decade; however, it is important to remember that legal judgments are only one component of how insurance companies price premiums. Insurers are financial institutions that earn profits from two sources, what they collect in premiums (less any payouts and other costs), and what they earn from investing the premium dollars they collect. Since insurers need to maintain significant cash reserves to cover expected costs and payouts, but these expenses occur at irregular intervals during a given year, they are able to "play the float" by investing their idle capital until it is required to fund operations. During the 1990s, financial markets were earning double-digit percentages each year, so insurers were able to more easily fund operations and judgments with the proceeds of their investments. With the coming of the bear market in 2000, insurers needed to make up the earnings shortfall from their other revenue source—premiums. As a result, malpractice premiums had to go up. Remember, though, that the increases were in many cases less about the size of malpractice judgments than about what was happening on Wall Street.

Are Americans Sicker?

One question that we increasingly hear relates to the overall health of Americans versus residents in other countries. This could manifest in two ways. Either Americans could have a higher rate of all diseases, or alternatively some higher-cost diseases could be more common in the United States. In January 2007 the McKinsey Global Institute released a study on U.S. health care costs, and it helped to address this question. The McKinsey researchers found that, overall, the United States looks a lot like the rest of the world with regard to its burden of disease. Some conditions such as obesity, anxiety, and early-stage prostate cancer are more common among Americans. On the other hand, other conditions such as hepatitis B, bladder cancer, and multiple myeloma are a bit less common in the United States. The bottom line—the United States incurs about $12 billion to $14 billion in additional health care costs because of its burden of disease. The conditions analyzed by the McKinsey team represented about 40% of all U.S. health care costs, so projecting their results up to the entire sum of health care costs gives us something in the range of $25 billion in extra annual expenses. While that sounds like a great deal of money, considered in the context of a U.S. health care system that now costs two trillion dollars each year to operate, the result is only about 1% of total expense.

Another analysis looked at Canada and its burden of disease in comparison to the United States and reached a similar conclusion. Since Canada is America's northern neighbor, and its life style, medical practice style, and culture are all relatively close to what we see in the United States, this analysis is probably an even better demonstration that the burden of illness just is not that different in the United States.

A more recent analysis by Kenneth Thorpe and his colleagues from Emory University, published in *Health Affairs*, reached a very different conclusion. They analyzed data from the OECD, CMS, and others to conclude that the prevalence of ten diseases was higher across the board in the United States than in Europe—in most cases considerably higher. This group also suggested that the treated prevalence (people who have been diagnosed and are receiving some sort of therapy) as well as medication use were also higher in the United States. They suggested that the more aggressive approach American doctors take to treating disease (something we will discuss in more depth later in this chapter) was part of the reason for the difference.

A May 2006 article describing a study comparing the relative health of middle-aged residents in the United States and the United Kingdom provides some support for Thorpe's position. This study was authored by Dr. James Marmot and his colleagues and was published in the *Journal of the American Medical Association*. It found that Americans were less healthy than their British counterparts with respect to a number of common diseases including high blood pressure, diabetes, heart attacks, strokes, and cancer.

The difference in methodologies may help account for the different results seen in these various studies, and a discussion of statistical niceties of each approach is well beyond the scope of this book. However, one thing we can say is that this is an area where independent researchers have reached conclusions that are almost diametrically opposed. As a result, we probably have to leave this particular topic as something of a question mark until more definitive data appear to support one or the other of these positions.

While there appears to be some controversy about the burden of illness in the United States versus the rest of the developed world, there is one place where there is agreement. Thorpe and his colleagues found that the obesity rate in the United States was almost twice what they saw in Europe. There is little question that the American obesity rate continues to escalate. A recent report from the Trust for America's Health stated 23% of Americans were now obese, and that Mississippi became the first state to achieve the dubious distinction of having 30% of its residents classified as obese. The report further stated that adult obesity rates have increased by more than one-third in the past quarter century. The linkage between obesity, diabetes, and cardiovascular disease is well known. While obese individuals will generally take a while to develop these complications, they are very likely to occur at some point. As a result, whether disease rates are or are not higher in the United States today, it does appear that they will be down the road, and this is likely to have a greater impact on future health care costs, making our current problem even worse.

Technology Access?

The term "medical technology" covers a lot of ground. In general, it can be defined as the procedures, equipment, and/or supplies which are used to deliver health care. All sorts of medical devices, pharmaceuticals, imaging equipment, and even innovative new ways of performing surgery are included. Americans tend to have something of a love/hate relationship with medical technology of various sorts. On one hand, it can be a significant driver of health care system effectiveness by allowing physicians and hospitals to do things that had not previously been possible, thereby saving and improving people's lives. On the other hand, new medical technology is almost invariably expensive and is widely agreed to be one key driver of health care costs.

Generally speaking, technology becomes a health care cost driver when one of two things happens. First, the technology can extend our lives. Most everyone would agree that is a good thing, and few would willingly give this advantage up. However, saving and extending our lives also gives us the chance to contract some other illness—which requires the use of still more health care resources—at some point in the future. The second way technology increases health care costs is when new inventions do not replace older tools, but instead become "add-ons." In medicine today, this is all too often the case. Technology is commonly developed for one use, and then later on is found to helpful for other uses as well. This happens frequently with technologies like prescription drugs, where doctors often find new uses for products. The question that matters most, and is often the hardest to answer, is whether or not new technology delivers good value for the money invested in purchasing it. Answering this question leads us to some of the most difficult ethical issues imaginable, like trying to value a human life and estimating the financial benefit of being free of various symptoms. These sorts of analyses are in the realm of health economists and outcomes researchers. Needless to say, some of the tools are very complex, and they are beyond the scope of this book. However, it is important to remember that medical technology has a cost, which we can usually understand pretty easily, and a benefit that can be much harder to calculate.

How much does technology diffusion contribute to the growth in U.S. health care costs? While there is wide agreement that it is an important factor, getting at the answer turns out to be very difficult. A 2001 analysis conducted by the Health Care Financing Administration (HCFA), the agency that was the precursor to CMS, used a "residual" method in an attempt to address the question. In other words, their researchers identified as many other factors contributing to health care cost growth as possible, backed out their influence, and attributed what was left (the residual) to the effect of new medical technology. The conclusion they derived from using this approach was that technology was responsible for somewhere between 40% and 70% of the growth in U.S. health care costs. The methodology of this analysis has been questioned by some, and other projections have suggested a lower level of contribution, more in the range of 10% to 40%. No matter which of these you choose to believe, technology is almost certainly an important factor in increasing health care costs.

Today, most medical technology is not country specific. New products that get invented in one part of the world generally tend to spread at some rate to other parts as well. There are regulatory issues for technologies like drugs, devices, and diagnostics that slow the rate at which technology can spread. Such products usually have to be proven to be safe and effective to the satisfaction of national regulators before they can be sold. However, in theory technology diffusion should affect all developed countries roughly equally over a period of several years.

As we have already briefly discussed, other countries tend to ration health care by limiting its supply. In other words, innovative technologies generally need to prove that they are more effective and, often, more cost effective than the older technologies they are designed to replace. In the United States, on the other hand, technology innovators are generally free to sell any new product once it has been demonstrated to be safe and effective.

Part of this difference in the approach to the use of new products is probably due to the different levels of interest in medical technology seen in the United States versus Europe. Minah Kim, Bob Blendon, and John Benson reported in *Health Affairs* in 2001 that Americans tended to be considerably more interested in new medical discoveries than were Europeans. Interestingly, this difference

"How much do you support or oppose the initiatives aimed at lowering the cost of your health care if it meant your access to new medical technology would be limited?"

(NET Support)	Health Plans	Employers	All MDs	Specialists	General Public	HDHP	Boomers	Seniors
Diagnostics and Imaging	55	31	26	25	26	34	27	26
Biologics/ Specialty Drugs	56	28	27	25	23	30	20	20
Intensive Care Unit	36	28	21	24	27	32	26	26

Figure 2.5 *Source*: **Harris Interactive, Strategic Health Perspectives 2007**

applied mostly to medical technology—it did not seem to carry through to technologies and scientific discoveries in other areas.

It is interesting to note that Americans have historically not been particularly tolerant of restrictions to technology. As part of its 2007 Strategic Health Perspectives service, Harris Interactive surveyed insurers/health plans, physicians, and the general public regarding their attitudes toward trading off access to modern technology in exchange for lower health care costs. The results are seen in Figure 2.5 and show that most groups in the United States would not support across-the-board restrictions on access to medicine's high-technology tools in exchange for lower costs.

By contrast, in recent years across much of Europe we have seen the rise of agencies designed to conduct what are often called "comparative effectiveness reviews." The United Kingdom's National Institute for Clinical Excellence (NICE) is one such body. It passes judgment on new pharmaceuticals and biotech products. It attempts to measure whether they provide sufficient "bang for the buck" and recommends whether or not the country's National Health Service should cover them.

It is also worth noting that in most of the rest of the developed world there are controls on the prices or profits of new technologies, especially pharmaceuticals. The case for such efforts is that they reduce costs for society as a whole and for individual patients. The argument against is that, by reducing profitability, such activities lower incentives for innovators to invest in new technologies to treat disease. The debate between these two philosophical poles is often quite heated. It is important to think about this critical question, because it has a great deal of potential impact on precisely what the health care system is actually able to offer patients, especially those suffering from poorly treated diseases. There is a direct relationship between the profits technology innovators can earn and the availability of such technology. As a result, while it is easy to complain about the cost of medical innovation, there is a trade-off between cost and access that we need to consider.

The United States has traditionally had a degree of distrust in the ability of governmental agencies or even independent national-level groups to make the sort of comparative effectiveness judgments that are common in Europe. Americans have generally been more comfortable with allowing markets to decide which new technologies are actually better than others. This process generally works, and it does let a lot of people participate in the decision-making process. However, it can be a bit messy and take some time.

There have been attempts in the United States to more formally regulate the spread of new medical technologies. The Certificate of Need (CON) laws passed by various states were one attempt to do so, especially with respect to health care facilities planning. Although the first CON law was passed in New York in 1964, they became more common as a result of the federal Health Planning Development Resources Act of 1974. According to the National Conference of State Legislatures, thirty-six states still have such laws on the books, despite the fact that the federal statute that spawned them was repealed in 1987.

The basic premise behind CON laws is that market forces do not work in health care as they do in other parts of the U.S. economy. In theory, excess construction of health care facilities leads to excess capacity and health care cost inflation. Supporters of CON tend to believe that, for example, if a hospital cannot fill all its beds, it charges higher prices for the beds that are used. By limiting construction of new beds, and the expensive equipment often required to support them, CON laws were supposed to restrict health care cost growth. It is not entirely clear whether or not CON laws actually worked as intended—the topic is still somewhat controversial. However, they did (and still do in many states) represent an attempt to limit health care cost growth by limiting the availability of hospital beds and the technology that often supports them.

Looking at comparative data from the OECD (shown in Figure 2.6), it does appear that the United States has a bit more high-tech imaging tools available that most of our comparison countries (Japan is the obvious outlier). Radiology and imaging costs are often expressed as part of hospital spending, since the technology is frequently located in the institutional setting. These costs are estimated to be in the range of $100 billion and have been growing at up to 20% per year. While $100 billion still represents only about a nickel of each dollar of health care spending, the growth is certainly a cause for concern. Interestingly, there is evidence that greater availability of radiology equipment is linked with higher spending on radiology services—a phenomenon called "supply-induced demand" that we will take up in more detail a little later on.

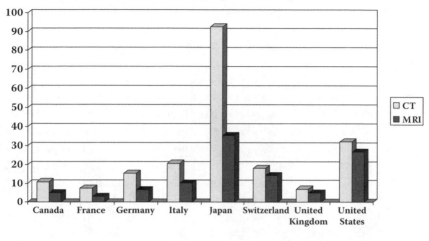

Comparative Availability of Imaging Technology
(Units Per Million of Population—2004)

(*=2002 Data)

Figure 2.6 *Source*: **Based on data from OECD Health Data**

With the rise of managed care in the United States over the past quarter century, we have seen other attempts to restrict access to technology. "Prior authorization" is the practice in which a physician or hospital is required to obtain approval in advance from an insurer before using some sort of test or treatment on a patient. This is enforced by the threat of nonpayment in the event that the provider fails to follow the insurer's rules. This tactic is typically applied to expensive interventions such as surgical procedures, referrals to specialists, medical devices, and to some prescription drugs as well. The effectiveness of these tools in controlling the cost of technology is also questionable. Physicians have viewed them as interference with their clinical judgment, and patients have seen them as barriers to care they thought they needed. Prior authorization programs are also relatively expensive for insurers to operate, and if the insurer winds up approving most of the requests that are made (which often turns out to be the case) having such a program in place can wind up not being cost effective. As a result, we have seen a slow decline in at least some of managed care's prior authorization programs over the past few years.

Perhaps the most effective efforts to restrict access to technology have been the formularies applied to limit the use of branded pharmaceuticals. For many years, drug costs were not really part of the national concern about health care spending. For example, there was no provision for drug coverage in the initial 1965 Medicare Act, because it was generally thought that the expense involved was not worth the bother. With the discovery of new product classes to manage previously untreatable diseases such as high cholesterol, mental illness, cancer, and others, pharmaceuticals began to become a more important part of U.S. medicine, and also of greater concern as a potential cost driver. As managed care began to dominate the payment mechanism for U.S. health care, tools such as formularies and differential copayments started to become more common.

The idea of a formulary, defined as restricted list of medications from which a physician can choose, dates back to the Revolutionary War. The concept was later applied primarily to hospital purchasing in an effort to help manage and control inventories. By the mid-1980s, with more and more Americans enrolled in managed care plans of various types, formularies started to become a tool to control prescription drug costs by limiting access. Managed care's original attempts at creating formularies often involved closed lists of drugs. Physicians and patients were simply unable to access drugs not on the list of approved medications without the patient picking up the entire cost of the prescription. Such restrictions understandably created backlash, especially when they seemed to be applied for economic rather than clinical reasons—which was often the case.

The next evolution of formularies was to make "nonpreferred" drugs available, but at a higher out-of-pocket cost to the patient. This turned out to be a master stroke. The insurer could legitimately claim that it was not restricting access to prescription products, but the patient wound up "self-rationing" if he or she was unwilling to come up with the extra money needed to pay for something other than the managed care plan's product of choice.

During this decade the concept of patient self-rationing has reached a new level with the advent of "three-tier" copayment models. In such plans, patients pay a relatively low price out-of-pocket (often $10 or less) to obtain a prescription for a generic drug. The managed care plan negotiates a discounted price with some pharmaceutical manufacturers who can in effect purchase a preferred formulary position in exchange for a significant price reduction. Patients typically pay $20 to $25 out-of-pocket to get a prescription for such a product. Products for which the manufacturer is unwilling to offer the managed care plan a discount go into a third tier, and patients must pay far higher amounts, often $30 to $40 per prescription to obtain them. In the past couple of years, the concept has been extended further as managed care plans have added a fourth tier for "lifestyle" products or very expensive specialty drugs such as injectable agents used to treat cancer or other rare diseases. Copayments for such products can often exceed $50 to $60 per prescription. The latest twist on this theme is "coinsurance." In such plans, the patient must pay not a fixed dollar amount, but rather a percentage of the products sale price. Since these four-tier plans are still relatively uncommon, we do not yet have a lot of data on their effectiveness, but if the past is any predictor of the future, it seems likely that they will be successful in further curbing the use of biopharmaceuticals.

Efforts have been quite effective. According to the Kaiser Family Foundation, the percentage of U.S. workers covered by three-tier/four-tier plans has risen to 71% in 2005, up from 27% in 2000. At the same time, the overall annual growth rate for sales of prescription drugs in the United States has dropped from 15% in 2000 to just 5% in 2005. Forcing patients into self-rationing has been quite successful in reducing spending growth; however, its effect on patient health has been less certain. In a July 2007 article published in the *Journal of the American Medical Association*, Dana Goldman of RAND Corporation and his coauthors stated that, for every 10% increase in patient cost sharing, prescription drug usage declined by 2% to 6%, depending on the drug class involved. For at least some chronic conditions, though, patients made greater use of other medical services. So, while formularies are effective at reducing drug spending by forcing patients to make choices about medication use, the larger question is whether or not patients are able to do this without creating more problems for themselves.

Medical technology does matter in terms of its effect on health care cost growth, and the difference between its impact on U.S. costs and costs in the rest of the world is largely defined by the effectiveness with which other countries use supply-side rationing to limit the rate at which new technology defuses. While we have tried to do some of same sorts of rationing in the United States, we have not been nearly as effective, and that is probably due in part to Americans' ongoing interest in and love affair with medical innovation. The one exception has probably been in prescription drugs, and this has been accomplished by financial "carrots and sticks" applied at the patient level. The question of whether or not patients are able to make such decisions without being "penny wise and pound foolish," though, remains open.

Moral Hazard?

"Moral hazard" is a term used frequently in the insurance industry. At the simplest level it can be defined as the risk that the presence of a contract will in some way affect the behavior of one of the involved parties. In the insurance industry this generally refers to the hypothesis that if you have a policy that covers you against a loss you may increase your risk-taking behavior.

In health care this concept has a couple of potential variations. First, there is a school of thought that suggests people with health insurance may not take care of themselves to the degree that someone without insurance might simply because they know they will not have to bear the full financial costs of their actions. Another variation of the moral hazard concept involves the idea that people who have health insurance will tend to consume more health care, especially unneeded care, than those without insurance because they do not have to pay the full cost of the services they receive out of their own pockets.

Moral hazard lies at the heart of the case for making patients more accountable for the costs of the care they receive. As its supporters would say, patients are fundamentally responsible for the decisions regarding their own health care. Since they are "overinsured," and do not face the economic consequences for their decisions, they are motivated to ask doctors for unnecessary care, and this is an important reason—possibly the most important reason—why health care costs so much in the United States.

These arguments are quite controversial. Opponents say that the health consequences of bad lifestyle decisions are not only financial. Shortening your life due to poor behaviors like smoking or overeating is at least as catastrophic as any financial consequences, and no form of insurance can protect against these noneconomic losses. In addition, health care procedures of various sorts have potential consequences that reach beyond economics. They take time, and they can be unpleasant or even dangerous for patients, and therefore they are not like buying a more luxurious car or a bigger home. Would people volunteer to undergo what the futurist Ian Morrison has called "recreational MRIs"?

So where does the truth lie? Unfortunately, good quantitative data are very hard to come by to support or refute either side of this case. Perhaps the simplest evidence comes from looking again at the health insurance systems of other countries. As we have already seen, nations like Germany, the United Kingdom, Canada, Italy, Japan, and Switzerland have universal health insurance coverage for their citizens, while the United States has about 15% of its population with no health insurance at all. These other nations generally make care available to their citizens at relatively low out-of-pocket costs at the time of service. If the moral hazard argument was completely correct, health care costs in these countries should be increasing faster than those in the United States, but this clearly is not the case. Utilization of health care services also does not suggest that moral hazard driven by low patient cost sharing necessarily increased use of medical services. Data from the OECD published in 2004 are shown in Figure 2.7. This suggests that United States residents already visit physicians somewhat less frequently than the OECD median. In other words, there does not seem to be an overinsurance phenomenon that is driving a lot of excess American patient visits.

What about more expensive items like surgical procedures? Figure 2.8 shows more data from OECD, and the results here are a bit more mixed. While there are somewhat more procedures performed in the United States than the OECD median, the United States is not a significant outlier and has a lower rate than

Average Annual Number of Physician Visits Per Capita in 2004

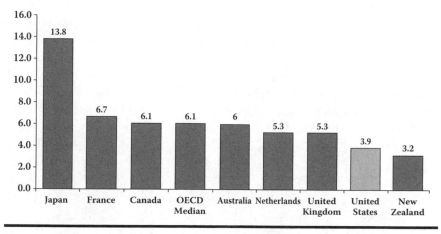

Figure 2.7   *Source*: Based on data from OECD Health Data

In-Patient Surgical Procedures Per 1000 Population (2002)

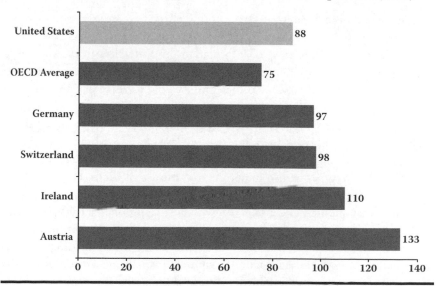

Figure 2.8   *Source*: Based on data from OECD Health Data

countries such as Germany and Switzerland, which we have already seen have lower health costs.

We also have seen, though, that these other health care systems limit the availability of new medical technology and use other forms of supply-side rationing, so the comparison may not be entirely fair.

To try to get a better answer to the potential role of moral hazard in U.S. health care costs, let us break this complex question down into a series of smaller parts that can addressed a bit more easily. First, are excess health care services delivered in the United States? Most experts would agree that there is overuse of at least some aspects of care. However, there is also wide agreement that we also have underuse of many important medical services.

In 2005, Elizabeth McGlynn and her colleagues from RAND Health published a now-famous paper in the *New England Journal of Medicine*. Dr. McGlynn found that American adults received the correct care (i.e., that recommended by medical experts) only about 56% of the time. In thirty-four of thirty-six care indicators discussed in the body of the paper, the problem was underuse rather than overuse. Overall, the authors concluded that underuse of health care was roughly four times as large a problem as overuse. On the other hand, the Agency for Healthcare Research and Quality (AHRQ) conducted research on the use of hysterectomies in women enrolled in seven different health plans and concluded that one in every six operations was inappropriate. AHRQ also found overuse of antibiotics and preoperative testing for cataracts. Since the 1970s Dr. John Wennberg and his colleagues at Dartmouth College have been researching variations in care delivery patterns in the United States. Their *Dartmouth Atlas of Health Care* is a treasure trove of information on differences in the way medicine is practiced in the United States. They have analyzed Medicare data from across the country and concluded there are twofold to threefold differences in per-beneficiary costs in different parts of the United States. After adjusting for the relative severity of illness in each geographic area, they concluded that a higher level of health care spending was not associated with any gain in life expectancy. Looking across all the evidence, it seems safe to conclude that there is significant overuse, but also underuse, and misuse of health care services in the United States today.

The second question to consider is if we have inappropriate health care delivered in the United States today, is this driven by patients? Unfortunately, it is extremely hard to separate the influence of doctors from that of patients in this question. My friend and colleague Humphrey Taylor from Harris Interactive offered this simple four-question test during presentations to a number of the firm's clients during 2007. Humphrey asked audiences:

1. How much inappropriate and unnecessary care is delivered to patients? (a lot, some, not much, none)
2. How many of you have ever asked for inappropriate or unnecessary care?
3. If you had a blocked artery and your cardiologist told you that you needed or would benefit from a drug-eluting stent, would you believe him or her?
4. So who should decide what is and is not appropriate? (the patient, the employer, the insurance company, the doctor)

Humphrey's amusing but thought-provoking questions cut to the heart of an important issue. Since 1966, the United States has operated under a legal principle called the "learned intermediary." This has been specifically applied to pharmaceutical and device companies, but the premise is actually quite broad. It states that, by warning doctors about potential problems with a medication, a manufacturer has discharged its responsibilities to patients as well. This is because doctors are trained to understand the scientific nuances and are also obligated to act in their patients' best interests. If you think about it, most of us go to visit a doctor when we have what we believe to be an important medical problem. That is because we understand that doctors receive extensive training in how to diagnose and treat health problems and are in the best position to make judgments about what health care we need. We do not always listen to our doctors, or follow their advice, but at least we generally recognize their superior knowledge. This is particularly true when we are scared or in pain—circumstances that frequently accompany being sick.

While it is certainly true that some patients do ask their doctors for specific health care products and services, doctors bear the ultimate legal responsibility for the services they provide. Because of the different knowledge levels between doctors and patients, it is also very hard for patients to really effectively critique their doctor's recommendations without the help of another doctor. The "second opinion" that patients sometime seek out before beginning a course of treatment is an example familiar to all of us. Given this knowledge gap between doctors and patients, and the dominant role that physicians play as the gatekeepers of most medical services, it seems a bit of a stretch to believe that the moral hazard of having insurance affects patients' behavior to such a degree that they demand a great deal of inappropriate health care and thus drive up health care spending in the United States. On the other hand, a strong case can be made that physician decision making plays a role in service utilization, and we will talk about how that happens in the next part of this chapter.

It is interesting to note that the moral hazard concept is most commonly applied to health insurance. Few people would suggest that average motorists drive more carelessly simply because they have a collision policy. Likewise, while there are occasional criminals who burn down their own buildings to collect insurance payments, this is certainly not the norm for most people who carry insurance on their homes. So why do we worry about this so much in health care?

As we said in Chapter 1, if you live long enough, it is highly likely that you will become a high user of health care. This is in contrast to other forms of insurance. Many people drive their whole adult lives and never file an insurance claim. Likewise most people who carry homeowner's insurance fortunately never have to use it. This difference between health insurance and other forms of insurance has led a number of people in the policy community to suggest what we really want when we buy health insurance is prepaid health care. There does seem to be some evidence to support this point of view, and that leads us back to the big questions we posed at the end of Chapter 1 about whether health care financing was a collective or individual responsibility. This difficult topic probably represents the ultimate moral hazard question. If you are young, healthy, and relatively well off economically, it is easy to believe that people who are old and sick are using insurance money that you helped to contribute in inappropriate ways. It is a short step from there to the belief that funding for one's health care in old age ought to come from money contributed during one's youth. That forms one of the ideological pillars for the current incarnation of consumer directed health care.

Waste, Fraud, and Abuse?

Opinion polls often find that members of the general public believe that these three little words drive an overwhelming amount of health care spending in the United States. Is this actually true? Like almost everything else in health care, the answer is very complex. Let us try to find an understandable explanation.

There is an old saying that, if there is one lawyer in a town, he or she will go bankrupt, but if there are two, they will get rich suing each other. We all see the grain of truth in this exaggerated characterization of the legal profession. There is an important underlying concept here, though, that does apply to health care—supply-induced demand. Remember that, in the discussion about moral hazard, we concluded that there was a significant asymmetry of information between doctors and patients that made it very difficult for patients to be a primary driver of excess use of health care services. If we turn this concept around, and look at it from the point of view of the medical community though, we see a very different picture. This needs to be accompanied by one of the most important thoughts in health care policy, namely, *"one man's waste is another man's revenue."*

We have mentioned the work of Dr. John Wennberg and his colleagues at Dartmouth College in the context of moral hazard. There are other and more important implications of this work. Dr. Wennberg has spent much of his career talking about supply-induced demand. By that, he means that the proliferation of medical technology (which we have already discussed) tends to produce pressure to use it, perhaps more often than is appropriate. In other words, physicians sometimes look at the marvelous tools they have available to them much like the shiny new toys children find under a Christmas tree—the temptation to play with them is almost irresistible. This is not to say that doctors are capricious or malicious in how they act, quite the contrary. Physicians and hospitals deal with people at their most vulnerable moments, and their actions can make the difference between life and death. However, providers also face some subtle influences regarding their use of health care services, many not of their own making, that do contribute to health care spending in the United States.

Back in the early 1990s, at the peak of our last health care crisis, it was common to go to policy meetings and watch a speaker take a pen in his or her hand, wave it in front of the audience and proclaim "this is the most expensive tool in all of medicine in the hands of a doctor." It is widely accepted that while physicians' services may only account for 20% to 25% of health care spending, their actions have a huge influence on much of what remains. The consensus among policy makers has generally been that physicians' actions (orders, prescriptions, admissions, etc.) account for roughly 80% of all health care costs in the United States.

U.S. physicians are trained to put their patients' interests first. When you sit in an exam room with your doctor, he or she is generally trying to figure out what is the best thing to do for you at that moment, regardless of the cost to society. In other words, if there is even a modest chance that a particular diagnostic test or treatment might do you some good (and is unlikely to hurt you), it is probable that your doctor will suggest that you get it. While this means that, as a patient, you can be confident that your doctor is acting on your behalf, it also represents a potential driver for health care costs.

There is a third element to consider, and that is how physicians get paid. In the United States today, medical reimbursement for physicians is overwhelmingly fee for service. What this means is that the more a physician does for patients, the more money he or she is likely to earn. While few in the health care policy community would seriously suggest that any substantive number of physicians provide more services to patients with the primary goal of enriching themselves, there is certainly the potential for some subtle influencing. Combine the greater availability of technology in the United States with the physician's goal of doing the best he or she can for an individual patient, then add in a system in which doctors who do more get paid more, and it is not hard to see where it all can lead.

Physician incomes in the United States have been falling when measured in terms of inflation-adjusted dollars. According to the Center for Studying Health System Change, physicians lost 7.1% of their inflation adjusted-income between 1995 and 2003. Flat or declining fees from payers were cited as the primary reason for this situation. Primary care physicians fared considerably worse than medical specialists. Given this downward pressure on incomes, the primary response of physicians has been to increase the volume and type of services they provide. This situation was highlighted in a 2004 article in *Health Affairs* by Robert Berenson and his colleagues. They described a physician move toward adding ancillary services, especially in imaging and laboratory testing, as well as physician investment in freestanding facilities to provide such services. The authors noted the challenges this activity creates for health care cost containment efforts. Obviously, such moves were easier for medical specialists to make than they were for primary care physicians, and that is at least partly reflected in the differences in income between the two groups.

It is very difficult to quantify exactly how big an effect on U.S. health care costs this situation has, especially because there is such a significant overlap with the technology access question we have already discussed. However, a number of health policy experts do see this as an important issue.

There are other ways to compensate doctors. During the late 1980s and early 1990s the United States had a brief fling with capitation. In concept, capitation is a bit like an "all you can eat" night at a local restaurant, except in reverse. A physician is paid a certain fixed amount per patient per month to provide a defined market basket of services for that patient. If the doctor is able to provide those services for less than the payment, he or she gets to keep the difference. If the doctor's costs exceed the payment received, the physician is responsible for the difference. This sort of payment mechanism obviously eliminates all physician incentives for overuse of medical care. So, what went wrong?

A number of problems led to the decline of capitation. First, there were concerns that physicians were being paid to undertreat patients, which put them in conflict with their obligations to them. Second, there were significant problems defining precisely what services were included and excluded from the market basket for which the physician received a fixed payment. Third, most physicians did not practice in medical groups large enough to tolerate the financial ups and downs associated with capitation. Finally, there was the problem of data. Neither the health plans that offered to capitate doctors nor the doctors themselves had sufficient information to be able to adequately understand the clinical implications of the compensation system.

Doctors can also be paid a salary. This eliminates incentives for both overuse and underuse. Unfortunately, it also eliminates incentives for doctors to see more patients, or be more productive. As one of the oldest jokes in health policy goes, "there are three ways to pay doctors, and all of them are wrong."

Hospitals have a different set of economic incentives. Until the early 1980s, hospitals were paid on a fee-for-service basis. They accumulated their charges, submitted the bill to insurers, and received payment in return. As hospital expenses grew, especially for Medicare patients, there was interest in seeing if an alternative could help contain cost growth. The answer was Diagnosis Related Groups (DRGs), which became the way in which HCFA paid hospitals. In brief, DRGs are a bit like capitation in that they are a form of prospective payment—a fixed payment defined in advance. Under DRGs, when a patient is hospitalized, he or she is assigned to one of roughly 500 groups that are expected to have generally similar patterns of hospital service use and, therefore, a similar pattern of costs. HCFA (and later CMS) assigns a payment amount for each group. If the hospital is able to provide care for less than that amount, it keeps the difference. If its costs exceed the DRG payment, the hospital absorbs a financial loss. DRGs and variations on them have now become the standard means by which all third-party payers, both public and private sector, now pay hospitals. This form of payment solves the problem of overuse, but it creates other problems. Hospitals spend a great deal of time and effort figuring out what the highest-paying DRG category is for each patient they admit. Not surprisingly, more complex cases get higher payments. Unfortunately, some of the reasons a hospital stay can become more complex are related to medical errors. For many years it was something of an open secret in the health policy community that hospitals could actually profit from at least some sorts of medical mistakes.

There are now attempts underway to find innovative ways to compensate both doctors and hospitals in the hopes of avoiding perverse incentives inherent in all current payment mechanisms. One of the most interesting is "pay for performance" (P4P). A P4P program involves identifying some outcome or process of interest, then rewarding performers for documenting that they have actually achieved the target. Not surprisingly, the bulk of P4P programs are targeted at physicians, and the sponsors include both private insurers and CMS. At the present time there are nearly 150 such programs in place in the United States. There are still a number of challenges associated with P4P. Defining exactly what sort of "performance" will be rewarded, putting in place the sort of information technology (IT) tools needed to adequately measure the performance, and putting sufficient rewards in place to motivate providers to pursue them are just some of the challenges P4P programs are now grappling with.

What about outright fraud and abuse? The National Health Care Anti-Fraud Association (NHCAA) defines fraud as "the deliberate submittal of false claims to private health insurance plans and/or tax funded public health insurance programs such as Medicare and Medicaid." What sort of impact does truly illegal behavior have on the cost of U.S. health care?

There is a widely cited study from the General Accounting Office (GAO) that goes back to 1994. It suggests that fraud and abuse make up perhaps as much as 10% of all U.S. health care spending. Private insurers generally estimate that fraud and abuse account for 3% to 5% of their claims. The NHCAA's own estimate is that at least 3% of U.S. health care spending in 2003 was due to outright fraud. Obviously, these sorts of actions are crimes and are aggressively investigated by the appropriate authorities. On balance, while 3% or so of health care spending is not a trivial amount, contrary to many "urban myths" it is not the primary driver of excess U.S. health care costs.

"Back Office" Costs?

It probably will not come as a surprise to anyone reading this book that not all the money spent on health care actually goes for the delivery of health care to patients. There are a myriad of support functions, many of which are involved with billings and collections, that are required to make the U.S. health care system operate. For many years, managed care plans have divided their proceeds into three categories: the amount needed to fund health care delivery (inelegantly referred to as the "medical loss ratio"), administrative expenses (including all the back office, billing, collection, IT, and support functions), and profits. Something similar happens for every major stakeholder in the health care system. How much money does all this "paper shuffling" require?

Estimates on this question vary considerably. Perhaps the simplest possible calculation is taken from the CMS National Health Expenditures database. It shows that in 2005 total U.S. health care spending was $1,987,689,000—a little less than two trillion dollars. Of this amount, CMS says that $1,661,372,000 was devoted to "Health Services and Supplies," which at first glance is roughly akin to the health plans' medical loss ratio and implies that about 83% of all health care spending goes to delivery of health care. CMS also lists $143,960,000, or about 7% of the total spent, for "Administration and Net Cost of Private Health Insurance." Unfortunately, CMS does not break out the billing and collections functions associated with doctor and hospitals. CMS also includes in its non-"Personal Health Care" numbers some things that are definitely not back office functions, like public health activity and research.

A 2002 paper by Steffie Woolhandler and David Himmelstein published in *Health Affairs* suggested that in 1999 U.S. administrative health care costs were roughly 25% of total U.S. spending in that year. As the argument made by supporters of a government-funded health care system goes, this spending is far higher than one sees in countries like the United Kingdom, and because it is not devoted to actual health care, that is a bad thing.

In its 2006 National Scorecard on U.S. Health System Performance, the Commonwealth Fund stated that total administrative costs in the United States were 7.3% of all health care spending. This contrasts with 5.6% in Germany, 4.8% in Switzerland, 3.3% in the United Kingdom, 2.6% in Canada, 2.1% in Japan, and just 1.9% in France.

There is another side to this story, though. Not all "administrative" expense is necessarily wasteful or unnecessary. Health care systems in the United States are large and complex. As we have already seen, there is a good deal of underuse, overuse, and misuse of resources. Clearly there needs to be some sort of management oversight exercised in order to try to address some of these potential problems. All of the IT costs needed to manage roughly one-seventh of the U.S. economy are also part of the "administrative" expenses. However, U.S. health care is almost certainly underinvested in IT. The average hospital will spend roughly 3% of its revenues on IT-related activities, which is about half of most American businesses invest and less than a third of the amount invested by information-heavy businesses such as banking. Similar conclusions can be drawn regarding IT expenses for physicians. Only 10% to 20% of U.S. physicians use electronic health records, and it is extremely difficult for physicians and hospitals to share even the minimal amount of electronic clinical information that is available. Poor coordination of care leads to a lot of wasted motion and misspent resources. One can make the case that, if we spent a bit more on at least some aspects of "administration," the nation's total health care bill might be lower.

In late 2005, James Kahn, Richard Kronick, Mary Kreger, and David Gans published an analysis of administrative health care costs in *Health Affairs*. While they were specifically looking at such costs for various stakeholders located in the state of California, they did conduct some analysis that can shed a bit of light on the national picture. They started with the Woolhandler/Himmelstein estimate that 25% of all U.S. health care spending was devoted to administration and tried to provide more detail by stakeholder, with a particular focus on how much was invested in getting money to flow through the system. For insurers, 9.9% was spent on administration, with another 8% devoted to billing and insurance related functions. For physicians' offices, the overall administrative ratio was 27%, with the billing functions consuming 14%—a bit more than half of the total. For hospitals, the total amount of administrative expense was 21%, with somewhere between 7% and 11% devoted to billing. Overall, the authors concluded that somewhere between 20% and 22% of all privately insured spending in California acute care settings was devoted to billing and insurance-related activities.

It is logical that, in the United States, our reliance on multiple private insurers does make the task of moving money around more complex. Each has its own forms to fill out and its own claims processing infrastructure. According to the McKinsey Global Institute report on U.S. health care costs, the United States spent $98 billion or $412 per capita on health care administration, and that amount was six times higher than the mean for all members of the OECD. Of this amount, fully $84 billion was attributed to private-sector insurers versus only $14 billion for all of Medicare and Medicaid combined. The public-sector programs are generally thought to spend no more than 3% to 5% of their budgets on administrative costs. The lower administrative costs of public-sector insurance appear to be replicated in other countries as well. The United Kingdom's National Health Service reportedly needs only 2% of its budget for administrative costs.

In fairness to U.S. private insurers, they do have to deal with expenses that public-sector programs do not have to face. For example, since insurers compete with each other for business, they need to have a sales and marketing infrastructure—something Medicare does not require. Private insurers are also often asked to take on tasks that are not generally considered part of the mission for public-sector programs. For example, during the 1990s when state Medicaid programs in the United States first began to turn to managed care as a means of containing cost growth, the health plans with which they contracted were often asked to put in place quality improvement programs. The efforts needed to develop, manage, and report on these sorts of activities are all part of the administrative cost burden that private insurers are asked to bear.

So administrative costs are high in the United States, and are higher than those seen in other countries. The added complexity of having multiple payers, each with different billing structures, is certainly a major contributor. However, not all administrative costs are bad, and the United States might actually benefit from greater investment in some areas. The key question is whether or not Americans are getting the best value for the money invested in administrative costs. At the moment, it would be difficult to answer that question with an unqualified "yes."

Is It the Prices?

In 2003, Gerald Anderson, Uwe Reinhardt, Peter Hussey, and Varduhl Petrosyan published an essay in *Health Affairs* entitled "It's the Prices, Stupid: Why the United States Is So Different from Other Countries." In it they suggested that

Percent of GDP Spent on Health Care vs. GDP per Capita OECD Countries

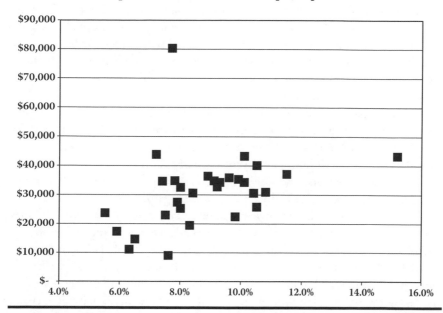

Figure 2.9   *Source*: **Based on data from OECD Health Data and International Monetary Fund**

the primary reason the United States spends so much more on health care than other countries is simply that the prices of everything associated with health care are significantly higher here than abroad. For example, over the past several years, Americans have become increasingly aware that there is a gap between the prices they pay for prescription drugs and the prices paid by Canadians and Europeans. That gap is been estimated to be in the range of 25% to 30%. Because Americans pay roughly a quarter of the bill for the pharmaceuticals (versus 10% for their doctor bills and just 2% for their hospital bills), this situation has attracted a lot of media attention. However, there is evidence that the "spread" for these other services is actually larger than that seen for drugs.

A good deal of data is available supporting the theory that the higher a country's GDP is, the more of that GDP it is likely to invest in health care. Figure 2.9 shows the relationship by plotting per capita GDP (adjusted to U.S. dollars and expressed in purchasing parity power) versus the percentage of national GDP devoted to health care for all members of the OECD. While the correlation does not fit that statistician's dream of a perfect diagonal line running from lower left to upper right, there is a clear trend to the data.

Anderson and his colleagues made an important point in their article. There are two factors contributing to total health care spending. The first is the units of service consumed (how many doctors' visits, prescriptions, hospital bed days, etc.), and the second is the price charged for each of those units. We have already seen that the United States is not a significantly greater consumer of either physician or hospital services than are other comparable countries. If Americans do not consume more units of these services than residents of other nations, then they must be paying more for each unit of service. The authors go on to suggest that one possible reason this happens is that in many other nations there is a single government agency that has the power to set prices, while in the United States, we have multiple private insurers, all of whom negotiate prices separately with providers, and none of whom represents a big enough share of those providers' revenues to really drive a hard bargain.

Admittedly, this is a controversial stance. However, other evidence does support at least the part of this hypothesis that talks about the United States versus rest of world price differentials. The McKinsey Global Institute report states that Americans pay $477 billion—28% of total U.S. health care spending—more than they should, due almost entirely to higher U.S. prices. Hospital care accounts for $224 billion of this amount, while all outpatient services account for the remaining $178 billion. The higher costs of nearly every input, including workers' salaries and supplies of various sorts, are a major contributor to this total. In a July 29, 2007, *New York Times* article, Alex Berenson points out that, despite all the pressure on their incomes over the past decade, U.S. physicians still earn two to three times as much as their colleagues in other developed countries.

The McKinsey study states that the difference in physicians' salaries accounts for $33 billion of the extra $178 billion that Americans spend on outpatient care. It goes on to point out, though, that the prices for hospital care are a far larger contributor to the greater spending seen in the United States. They point out that the cost of a day in a U.S. hospital bed averages $1,611 versus $862 for Denmark, which is the next closest developed nation. The average for the entire OECD is only $338. The United States consumes fewer hospital bed days than do other developed nations, so this erases some of the price gap, but the total per capita cost of hospitalization in the United States is still nearly two times higher than the second-ranked nation and almost three times the OECD average.

Before deciding the U.S. physicians are simply overpaid, it is important to note that the cost of becoming a physician in the United States are also much greater than comparative costs in most of the rest of the developed world. As the Congressional Research Service noted in a September 2007 report on health care costs, nearly 90% of all new U.S. medical graduates left school with educational debt averaging almost $130,000. This contrasts with what is common practice in most of Europe, where education is highly subsidized or even free to students.

This raises some interesting questions. Given that most new doctors start their working lives with significant debt and half of the cost of hospital care is made up of the wages of the people who work there, are we really interested in reducing their paychecks as a way of lowering our health care costs? These are the people we turn to when we are at our most vulnerable. In general most people would probably agree that they would like to see enough economic incentives to encourage our "best and brightest" to go into medical professions. However it is also fair to ask "how much is enough?" Are there lower-paid workers, like nurse practitioners or physicians' assistants, who can pick up more of the work load traditionally carried by physicians? Can health care follow the model of other industries and begin to make better use of technology to improve the productivity of its expensive workers? There may not be an easy way to "have our cake at eat it too," but given the importance of the answer, we owe it to ourselves to try.

So, what have we learned about U.S. health care's "usual suspects?" Aging populations and malpractice judgments may be cited often in the popular press, but there is little evidence to show they are major contributors to either the overall costs of U.S. health care or the difference between costs in the United States and elsewhere. The evidence regarding the burden of disease in the United States is more varied, but at some point in the future, if the U.S. obesity epidemic continues, this will almost certainly become a much bigger challenge. We have also seen that the moral hazard argument—that U.S. residents are overinsured and as a consequence demand a great deal of unnecessary care—does not have a lot of evidence to support it. On the other hand, issues related to health care's "supply side" such as physician behaviors, more open access to technology, administrative costs, and higher U.S. prices have a great deal to do with explaining the higher costs of the U.S. system. Health care in the United States is also very fragmented and poorly coordinated, often because physicians are unable to easily communicate with each other about a particular patient's treatment. This is another consequence of the U.S. health care system's underinvestment in the IT tools that could address this problem. Provider financial incentives and pressures on physician incomes only add to the challenges we face. The big question emerging from this exploration of reasons for U.S. health care costs is "who is best positioned to tackle these problems?" Keep this question in mind as we turn to our discussion of consumer directed health care.

Chapter 3

Consumer Directed Health Care

Back in early 2003, I had what I thought might be my first encounter with serious illness. I had some gastrointestinal problems that were suggestive of a whole range of potential diagnoses that ranged from trivial to life threatening. I went to visit my primary care provider, who made a presumptive diagnosis (gastrointestinal reflux disease), but also wanted me to see a specialist just to be sure. Because he told me that it might take a while to get an appointment with the specialist, he also prescribed a proton pump inhibitor to relieve my symptoms. The next day, I called the specialist to make an appointment and learned it would be approximately three months before there was an opening. In the meantime, I took my medication, and my symptoms improved. When I finally did see the gastroenterologist, he suggested that actually I needed *two* endoscopies—one for my upper GI tract to see what was causing my initial symptoms and a colonoscopy because I was on the wrong side of 50 and needed a baseline evaluation. He booked me for two separate dates roughly six weeks later.

At the first appointed date (for the colonoscopy), I arrived at my local hospital about two hours before the time scheduled for the procedure. I went to the outpatient treatment center, checked in, and for the rest of the morning I became part of America's medical bureaucracy. I was wheeled from one floor to another and eventually got to the endoscopy suite, where I again saw the gastroenterologist. When I woke up roughly half an hour later, I was on my way back to the recovery room. My wife sat with my doctor and got the good news that at least the lower half of my GI tract was normal. A week later, I returned and went through almost an identical process, including giving exactly the same medical history and insurance information to exactly the same woman. I once again fortunately found that the other half of my GI tract was completely normal—if there had been any problems present, the medication had long since healed them.

When all this was over, I called my family care provider and gave him the news—as a veteran of health care, I made no assumption that he and the gastroenterologist would talk about my case or that any records would pass from the hospital where I had been examined to my primary care provider. To the best of my knowledge the two never did speak.

Several weeks later, I learned that there was no medical reason why I had to go to the hospital twice for these examinations. Once I was adequately anesthetized, both procedures could have been done in one sitting, and I could have been finished with the entire process in a single day. The convenience of the hospital staff, the gastroenterologist, and the extra reimbursement the hospital got from admitting me twice were the primary reasons why my situation was handled in the way it was. To this day, I still scratch my head over the time it took to get the care delivery system to focus on me—almost five months from end to end. In hindsight, I am very grateful I did not have a serious problem. All the nurses and doctors I encountered treated me wonderfully; it just was not what anyone would call a "patient-centered" process. There is another message here as well; despite my many years working on the inside of health care, and my knowledge of health policy, the system still got the better of me. Making good decisions is hard, especially when you do not have all the information you need, and getting that information is a real chore even for people with expertise in the field.

In contrast, earlier this year another member of my household had another and, as it turned out, far more serious medical problem. My eleven-year-old Burmese cat, Godiva, had been slowly losing weight for several months. My veterinarian and I had tried a couple of tricks to get her to eat more, but it was not working out. One morning, Godiva, a cat that had always been extremely fastidious about using her litter box, left a little "present" on my wife's bathroom throw rug. There appeared to be some blood in the feces, so as soon as my vet's office opened, I called. My vet referred me to a secondary veterinary group about 30 miles away that had far more sophisticated diagnostic tools than she did. Within about two weeks we were able to agree on a presumptive diagnosis (cancer), discuss therapeutic options, and settle on a treatment plan (surgery). I had little problem communicating with all the various veterinary specialists; they had access to all the data they needed to advise and were very open about sharing it with me. The speed with which my little cat moved through the process was breathtaking. I am happy to report that this story also had a happy

"Godiva"

Figure 3.1

ending. While Godiva did have the feline version of colon cancer, her surgeon was able to remove the tumor entirely, and I got a very impressive pathology report from a local university telling me that the surgeon had indeed gotten the entire tumor and there had been no spread to the cat's lymph nodes. Godiva came home and has made a remarkably full recovery. In the course of just three weeks, we went from symptoms to diagnosis to treatment (Figure 3.1).

The comparison between these two situations reveals some pretty stark differences and speaks eloquently to the fact that the United States can deliver "patient-centered" care when it wants to; it just does not do a particularly good job of it for two-legged patients. I suspect that many of you reading this book have your own versions of my story. I will ask you to bear these stories in mind as we move through our discussion of consumer directed health care and my suggestions for improvements.

Apparently my experience really is not unique. There is considerable support in the policy community for making our system more "consumer-centric." In March 2001 the Institute of Medicine issued its seminal report on U.S. health care entitled *Crossing the Quality Chasm*. This report described in considerable detail many of the failings of U.S. health care and called for a system that was safe, effective, efficient, equitable, timely, and personalized—later abbreviated as STEEEP. This acronym has spread widely through the health policy community and is now generally considered one of the "articles of faith" when the subject of health care reform is discussed. The Institute further went on to define patient-centric care as "health care that respects and honors patients' individual wants, needs, and preferences, and that assures that individual patients' values guide all decisions." In April 2006, the Commonwealth Fund released the results of a survey, published in the *Archives of Internal Medicine*, showing that, although large majorities of physicians supported patient-centered care principles, only about 22% of U.S. physicians actually practiced that way.

It seems only a matter of semantics to move from "patient-centered" to "consumer directed," but that is not the case in the United States today. In fact, the two terms have very different practical meanings, and to learn about the "consumer directed" portion of the equation, we need to turn the clock back about ten years.

By the mid-1990s, it was increasingly obvious that the first generation of managed care was under stress. The Clinton health care reform plan, which relied heavily on managed care, was in ruins. Consumers, who in many cases had been forced into various manifestations of managed-care plans by their employers, were beginning to rebel against what they saw as heavy-handed restrictions on their access to medical care. In many cases, the physician community was a major contributor to this consumer angst as doctors talked with their patients about the care they were unable to provide due to various managed-care cost-containment measures. The mainstream media took up the cause, and managed care's "death by anecdote" was underway. Employers began to back away from health maintenance organizations, the most restrictive form of managed care, and the insurers themselves began to back away from the cost-containment tools that had made them effective, but also so unpopular in such a short period of time.

Not surprisingly, after a few years without a strong voice for cost containment coming from the demand side, health care spending rates once again started to explode, as Figure 3.2 shows. By the beginning of the millennium, it was starting to look as though health care insurance rate increases were on their way back to the historic peaks seen in 1989. As we discussed in Chapter 1, rate increases of this sort are intolerable to employers, especially when they are unable to raise prices for their consumers. However, employers and managed-care organizations had no wish to rerun the public relations fiasco of the previous decade. In addition, it was increasingly apparent that much of managed care's early initial success had been due to its ability to demand significant price discounts from a fragmented provider market. Throughout the later half of the 1990s hospitals had engaged in aggressive consolidation strategies. This largely happened in response to pressure from managed care. Newly merged providers had managed to increase their negotiating leverage with managed care, thus making it unlikely that the price discounting approach could work a second time.

At this point, the strategy that most of the payer community began adopt was best described by Humphrey Taylor as "let them eat choice." If consumers rebelled at restrictions on access to care, this time the payer community would make almost all forms of care accessible, but at a price. As we have already

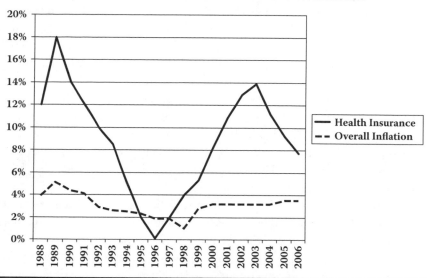

U.S. Health Insurance Premium Increase Rates vs. Inflation

Figure 3.2 *Source:* **Henry J. Kaiser Family Foundation**

discussed, prescription drugs were an early target through multitier formulary plans where consumers had to make the decision about how expensive they wanted their medications to be. Copayments for physicians and hospitals also started to increase dramatically as managed care started building on the success it had seen with drugs. Insurers and employers could legitimately claim, with at least some justification, that they were not hampering consumer access to the delivery system and all of its technologic marvels. By shifting costs to consumers, they were also able to help minimize the rate at which their own expenses climbed and thereby relieved at least some of the economic pressures they faced. However, this approach lacked a unifying principle. It also had a finite end, because the general expenses of many higher-end health care services were clearly beyond the ability of most Americans to afford. With median household incomes in the United States in the range of $45,000 to $50,000, a single day in a hospital bed cost more than a week's after-tax pay.

A little-noted provision in the 1996 Health Insurance Portability and Accountability Act (HIPAA) provided a part of the answer. Along with its much better known provisions concerning the privacy of health information, this act also authorized a private-sector demonstration project of a novel health care financing vehicle known as a medical savings account (MSA). Medical savings accounts borrow heavily from the self-funded defined-contribution retirement accounts, 401(k)s, that had started to spread through the employer market back in the early 1980s. An MSA is a savings vehicle, much like a 401(k), and the new provisions of HIPAA made contributions to MSAs tax-exempt. The difference between the two is that withdrawals can be made at any time from an MSA to pay for authorized health care expenses, while penalty-free withdrawals from a 401(k) are off limits until the account holder is at least 59½ years of age. In 1997, a provision in the Balanced Budget Amendment (BBA) authorized a similar limited demonstration project for Medicare. Medical savings accounts were marketed by several firms, one of the most notable of which was the Golden Rule Insurance Company located in Indianapolis. Despite the congressional encouragement, MSAs struggled to gain market acceptance, and only about 50,000 had been purchased by the start of 1999.

A politically conservative Texas economist named John Goodman provided a much-needed spark. He had been developing and pushing a concept that borrowed from the themes of individualism, cost shifting, and MSAs. Goodman is generally credited with developing the concept of marrying a new type of health insurance, one that would carry an extremely high deductible, with a tax-deferred savings vehicle and dubbing it "consumer directed" health care. The National Center for Policy Analysis (NCPA), where Goodman now works, has a Web site containing a number of materials relating to his activities. These suggest that the underlying concepts go back a number of years and can be attributed to a number of economists. They further describe the efforts of its supporters to stimulate the pilot projects described above and the subsequent efforts to make consumer directed health care part of mainstream health policy thought. In brief, the intellectual precepts of consumer directed health care are:

- Health care and its financing is primarily an *individual* rather than a *societal* problem—it is a market good, available to people who can afford it, rather than any sort of "right." The funding for the higher expected expenses later in life should be paid for in advance from earnings during one's working years.
- Consumers are overinsured. Since they do not bear the primary brunt of the economic consequences associated with their choices in health care, they do not exercise good judgment with respect to health care purchasing, and they ask for excessive/unnecessary health care. If consumers have a significant personal financial stake in their health care choices, they will exercise better judgment. This consumer empowerment will be the tool to contain health care costs and will succeed where organized purchasers (such as managed care and CMS) have failed.

■ Consumers are competent to manage their own medical care and are interested in doing so. They will seek out and use information on price and quality to make medical decisions and will do so wisely.

It is important to draw a clear distinction between a *high-deductible* health plan (HDHP) and the newer *"consumer directed"* plans (CDHPs). The important difference between the two is the addition of the tax-sheltered savings account. As we will see, there is still a great deal of confusion, even in policy circles, between CDHPs and HDHPs. From this point onward, I will try to explain which one of these two we are talking about as we go through our review.

The CDHP concept had a considerable intellectual appeal for a number of important stakeholders in health care, and not surprisingly, it attracted a good deal of initial support.

For ideological conservatives, it was an opportunity to offer a new idea in a field traditionally dominated by the political left, and it came at a time when there was little new thinking emerging from that part of the ideological spectrum following the failure of the Clinton health care plan. It allowed conservatives to say something innovative about health care, while still working to minimize the role of the federal government in controlling health care, as well as potentially also advancing their tax-cutting agenda.

For the provider community, CDHPs seemed to provide the opportunity to get out from under managed care and the downward pressure it had exerted on pricing, by turning the entire demand-side responsibility over to individual consumers. A similar attitude was expressed by suppliers of tools like medical devices, diagnostics, and pharmaceuticals, who had also seen the impact of managed care on their business and hoped to be able to deal more directly with patients.

Consumer directed health plans still maintained the role of private insurers in providing actual policies. They also eliminated much of an insurer's responsibilities performing the often-unpleasant tasks of managing the demand side of health care. The ultimate vision of CDHP's advocates was to transform insurance from a product purchased for large groups by powerful employers to a product purchased by individuals. While this might increase an insurer's marketing costs (reaching out to millions of people costs more than enrolling them through the workplace), these costs could be more than offset by savings elsewhere and by new services that could be offered to consumers. As a result, the idea was very popular among the insurance community as well.

A significant percentage of employers were also initially very supportive of the CDHP concept. Rising health care costs were forcing many of them to rethink their roles as health insurance providers, and a number were starting to conclude that buying health insurance simply was not a core competence of their business. Consumer directed health plans gave them the opportunity to move a large portion of these costs off their income statements by handing them off to their employees. It also took them out of the business of saying "no" to employees who were seeking medical care by making those employees the decision makers. Perhaps most importantly, it gave employers an opportunity to insulate themselves from future health care cost increases.

Interest also came from an unlikely corner—the financial services industry. With the end of the long bull stock market in 2000, many investment firms and banks were beginning to look for new sources of revenue. Since these firms had experience with 401(k) accounts, they already had the skills required to manage the financial aspects of the associated savings accounts, an expertise that insurance companies lacked.

Finally, there were supporters among selected groups of consumers as well. Generally speaking, these included younger, healthier, economically advantaged individuals who did not believe that they were likely to experience significant health care problems and for whom deductibles of several thousand dollars a year would not be a significant financial burden. These individuals were further intrigued by the prospect of being able to shelter more income (that contributed to the health savings account) from taxation, thereby creating what amounted to a second retirement savings account.

The most obvious group missing from this list of supporters were typical consumers with average household incomes and a normal distribution of medical problems. Humphrey Taylor conducted an informal poll among attendees at the inaugural World Health Care Congress meeting held in January 2004. Humphrey asked attendees to indicate by show of hands who was the primary force behind consumer directed health care. None of the audience, which included some of health care's most influential policy makers, indicated that they thought consumers had played any significant role in the process. Rather, their votes suggested that employers and insurers, instead of consumers, had been primarily responsible for the success consumer driven health care had enjoyed to that point. This informal poll did not necessarily suggest a disparagement of the principles of consumer directed health care or disagreement with its precepts. However, it does suggest that referring to these plans as "consumer directed" might be somewhat less than accurate.

Several small entrepreneurial firms, such as Definity Health (founded in 1998—purchased by United Health Care in 2004) and Lumenos (founded in 1999—purchased by WellPoint in 2005), entered the health insurance marketplace with CDHP packages that combined an insurance plan carrying a very significant deductible and a high out-of-pocket annual cap with various savings vehicles. These pioneers represented the first substantive commercialization of the consumer directed health care movement.

December 2003 represented a real turning point for CDHPs as the Medicare Modernization Act (MMA) was signed into law. This law involved a series of compromises between Democrats and Republicans, driven by substantial time and budget constraints as well as a shared desire to "do something" for senior citizens by extending Medicare coverage to include prescription drugs. Although the "Part D" program for pharmaceuticals got most of public's attention, this new law also changed the MSA into a health savings account (HSA). It further affirmed the tax deductibility of contributions and formally coupled them to high-deductible insurance policies. The legal provisions of consumer directed health care were now in place.

More than anything else, the MMA broadened the scope for these new vehicles. Where the previous MSA demonstration project had been limited to self-employed individuals or companies with less than fifty employees, the new consumer directed health care plans were available to anyone. The MMA further sharpened the definitions of the accompanying high-deductible insurance policy. Under the new law, such a policy needed to carry a minimum deductible of $1,000 per individual or $2,000 per family. The deductibles were indexed for inflation so they increase each year. It set an annual cap on out-of-pocket expenditures at $5,000 for an individual and $10,000 for a family. Finally, it set contribution limits for the HSA of $2,600 for an individual and $5,150 for a family. In 2007 Congress tinkered a bit further with the formula for the HSA contribution level, raising it to $2,850 for an individual and $5,650 for a family. Finally, the MMA established a "safe harbor" for preventative care. This would be exempted from the high initial deductible, meaning that an insurer could offer full coverage for this sort of care without running afoul of the new rules.

There was also one final variant to the savings account vehicle, and this slightly preceded MMA. A number of employers had expressed reticence about the HSA. An HSA is fully owned by the employee, much like a 401(k), and is portable, meaning that if the employee changes jobs the HSA moves along with him or her. Some employers were looking for an intermediate vehicle—one they could fund themselves and also help to control. Many wanted the ability to have the funds stay with the company if the employee departed. Some were also interested in having more control over the types of expenses for which the balance in the account could be used. The fix was the Health Reimbursement Arrangement (HRA). The HRA was first officially blessed by the IRS in June 2002 and clarified by a series of subsequent refinements.

An HRA account looks a good deal like the HSA from the point of view of the employee, but offers the tradeoff of employer funding in exchange for the loss of portability. HRAs are what are called in accounting-speak "notional accounts." In plain English, that means that an employer puts aside a total amount of money for a category of expenses and sets a cap on the amount that can be devoted to any particular individual, but there are no actual "accounts" assigned to any specific person. This has the effect of increasing the employer's flexibility with regard to spending. It also means that the tax deduction for expenses associated with an HRA remains with the employer rather than accruing to the individual on whose behalf the employer actually spent funds. An HRA must be fully funded by the employer (no accompanying salary reductions), and it must be used to pay only for "substantiated medical expenses." HRAs may also roll over balances from year to year. As long as these criteria are met, the IRS grants HRAs tax-sheltered status.

So, let us summarize how consumer directed health care plans work today.

■ First—there is an insurance plan that covers catastrophic medical expenses. If such a policy covers an individual, in 2007 there is a mandatory deductible of $1,050. If the policy covers a family, the mandatory initial deductible is $2,100.

■ Second—if policy holders exceed the initial deductible amount, they continue to have some degree of financial liability, in the form of either copayments or coinsurance up to a limit of $5,250 (individual) or $10,500 (family).

■ Third—two types of savings accounts are associated with the high-deductible insurance policy—an HRA or an HSA. HSAs belong to an individual, and contributions are tax deductible up to a limit of $2,850 (individual coverage) or $5,650 (family). Outside contributions, such as those that might be made by an employer, are allowed within the established limits. Withdrawals from an HSA can be made at any time for any authorized health expenditure. Health savings accounts are portable. If an individual owning an HSA changes jobs, the HSA balance moves with the person. In contrast, an HRA is entirely funded by an employer, who retains any tax deduction associated with the account. There is no upper limit on the size of an HRA, and it can be used to pay for any health-related expense authorized by the employer. However, if an employee changes jobs, he or she loses any remaining funds available in the account. Both HSAs and HRAs have rollover provisions, meaning that if there is a balance remaining in the account at the end of the year, the amount carries over to subsequent years. Account holders can therefore use the accounts to "save up" for an elective procedure in the future. If the amounts accrued in an HSA are not spent on health care, they can be withdrawn by the account holder at age 59½ for any purpose without incurring a tax penalty, meaning that they can be used as a second IRA for people able to contribute significant amounts to them each year.

- Fourth—there is an exemption from the deductible for "preventative care." This term was vaguely defined by Congress in the MMA, but subsequent IRS rulings have clarified the meaning of preventative care to include early detection and prevention of disease. Generally speaking, this does not include costs associated with the treatment of any existing illness.
- Fifth—almost all plans claim to offer various information support tools for consumers that are supposed to provide information on cost and quality to assist consumers with decisions making. Most of these tools are Web based. As we will see when we talk about issues associated with consumer directed health care later, due to a set of much larger health policy issues, there is actually quite a bit less here than meets the eye.
- Finally—a number of consumer directed health plans also offer various "wellness" programs designed to help enrollees manage lifestyle issues such as smoking cessation, exercise, and weight loss. Some also offer "disease management" programs, which generally consist of a nurse case manager who deals directly with patients over the phone and offers advice to them on various issues associated with care of chronic conditions.

The RAND Health Insurance Experiment— Impact on Consumer Directed Health Care

Despite the high-level interest in consumer directed health care (a high-deductible insurance plan coupled with an HSA or an HRA) from many stakeholders, these vehicles have been controversial almost from day one. Probably one of the biggest objections has been the concern that the high-deductible insurance plan would encourage consumers to avoid medical care that they should be receiving—a theme we will explore in more detail later on.

Both advocates and opponents of consumer directed health care routinely cite an experiment in health insurance conducted by RAND Corporation in the 1970s as support for their views. As we start exploring what we do and do not know about consumer directed care, it is important to turn to a rather arcane part of health policy lore to understand what this project does, and does not tell us, and how that knowledge can be applied to the current U.S. health care system.

In 1971, RAND Corporation received funding from the U.S. Department of Health, Education, and Welfare—a precursor of the current Department of Health and Human Services. These funds were applied to answer a number of questions that were then becoming more interesting for the nation's policy community. Perhaps the most important of these was "does health care that is free to the patient at the point of delivery lead to better health outcomes than care where the patient must pay part of the cost?" This question was important to the Nixon Administration, because one of the numerous waves in support of health care reform was starting to build, and the president was interested in having support for a private-sector marketplace. RAND next set up something roughly like an insurance company with its federal grant and then recruited roughly 7,700 people to participate in the experiment. These individuals were randomly assigned to five different groups of roughly equal sizes. One group faced no out-of-pocket spending to receive health care. Three other groups faced 25%, 50%, and 95% coinsurance rates with an annual cap on out-of-pocket spending of $1,000—a relatively large sum at the time and in the general range of the out-of-pocket caps for today's high-deductible policies expressed in inflation-adjusted dollars. The amount was scaled back for low-income participants. The final group was assigned to a staff model health maintenance organization (HMO), the Group Health Cooperative of Puget Sound based in Seattle, Washington. The groups were then compared for utilization of medical services and medical outcomes. The RAND Health Insurance Experiment kicked off in 1973 and concluded in 1982. It is still the largest and longest controlled experiment on the effects of health insurance cost sharing.

A huge amount has been written over the past twenty-five years regarding the RAND Health Insurance Experiment and its findings. Literally hundreds of publications have examined its implications. While there were a number of findings, three are particularly important in the debate over consumer directed health care.

The first seems logical—participants who were asked to pay more for health care used less of it. In economic terms, this means that demand for health care is "elastic," meaning that it increases and decreases relative to the price charged for it. This finding is often quoted by supporters of high-deductible insurance to show that cost shifting can reduce health care cost growth.

The second is somewhat less obvious—participants cut back on care deemed to be "necessary" and "unnecessary" in roughly equal proportions. Furthermore, the cost savings consumers achieved in the higher cost-sharing groups came from lower utilization of services rather than from consumers shopping around for lower prices. In other words, consumers were not particularly good decision makers about when to reduce their consumption of health care, nor were they price shoppers. It is also noteworthy that the cost-sharing burdens in the RAND experiment did not induce consumers to take better care of themselves. Behaviors such as obesity and smoking occurred in equal proportions in all groups. These results are often quoted by opponents of high-deductible health care to suggest that such policies are potentially dangerous to consumers who are not especially sophisticated about health care.

The final finding is perhaps the most controversial of all—although participants cut back on both needed and unneeded care in equal proportions, there was no significant difference in outcomes between any of the groups. There were some important exceptions. People who were poor or sick generally did experience negative outcomes associated with having to pay more out of pocket for their care. This finding has been quoted (and misquoted) by both opponents and defenders of consumer directed health plans in the years since it was first published.

Much has been extrapolated from the RAND Health Insurance Experiment over the past two decades, and the degree to which its lessons can be applied to the current health care environment in the United States is probably more limited now than in the 1980s. Medical science has advanced considerably. For example, the RAND experiment concluded several years before the introduction of statins, the first effective and patient-acceptable products to lower cholesterol. The RAND experiment was also conducted at a time when the U.S. health care system was still primarily focused on the management of acute events. Since that time, the burden of chronic diseases with their need for lifelong management and a team approach has grown, as has our knowledge of how best to control them. As is almost always the case with scientific experiments, the RAND findings leave us with a number of questions that we wish we could go back and address. Unfortunately, we are left with the findings we have rather than the findings we would like to have.

Effects of Consumer Directed Health Care

As satisfying as it would be to say that the results of the RAND experiment have (or have not) been confirmed by the emergence of consumer directed health care into the market place, it is simply too early to make many conclusions. While the supporters and critics are quick to extrapolate from anecdotes or from "hired gun" self-serving research studies, we are going to stick to evidence from independent sources and limit ourselves to what the data actually demonstrate. We will rely heavily on three sources. The primary one is Harris Interactive's Strategic Health Perspectives survey. This is proprietary data collected from polling a number of health care stakeholders including the general public, enrollees in CDHP and HDHPs, baby boomers, senior citizens, doctors, employers, and health plan executives. Since Harris Interactive has been doing these surveys for a number of years, we can use their data to get some idea about trends over time. The other data sets we will use look specifically at CDHPs, and both were completed at the end of 2006. These come from two independent and highly respected organizations, the Henry J. Kaiser Family Foundation and the

Commonwealth Fund. The Commonwealth Fund's survey was conducted in conjunction with the prestigious Employee Benefits Research Institute. Each of these data sources looked at slightly different aspects of consumer directed health care, so while there is considerable overlap in the three surveys, they do not always match up perfectly in terms of how the questions were worded or the areas they covered.

We will use other data to fill in the blanks when our three primary sources do not give us the information we need. For example, the Henry J. Kaiser Family Foundation conducts an annual survey on employer-sponsored health care, and this is widely considered to be a definitive source of information about what employers are doing with respect to health insurance. We have already seen a little of the information this survey provides in the chart that shows the increase in health care premiums versus the increase in the overall rate of U.S. inflation. We will refer to some studies from the insurance industry itself, but readers need to bear in mind that the these sources generally have a very strong vested interest in the outcome of any survey they conduct, so their data need be viewed through that filter.

Enrollment

How many people are enrolled in consumer directed health plans? An April 2007 report from the health insurance industry's trade association, AHIP, stated that as of January 2007, 4.5 million people were enrolled in such vehicles, up from 3.2 million the year before, and up significantly from the roughly 1.1 million reported in March 2005. AHIP further reports enrollment growth coming from both the employer-sponsored market and the individual market. The data are shown in Figure 3.3. What is perhaps a bit troubling is that, with all the attention devoted to high-deductible health plans over a period of nearly ten years, total enrollment still represents less than 2% of the total U.S. population, and less than 2% of total number of Americans with health insurance.

It is also very important to note that there is some controversy concerning whether or not these enrollees are in true "consumer directed" plans (with a spending account) or just high-deductible policies. While the AHIP survey implies that all these enrollees do have either an HSA or an HRA, other surveys provide a very different picture. The Harris Interactive SHP survey of CDHP/HDHP enrollees suggests only 17% of those with a high-deductible plan have an HSA, and only an additional 8% have an HRA. These percentages were unchanged from 2006. A survey conducted in January 2007 by the Vimo Research Group suggested that less than one-third of the 3 million enrollees claimed by AHIP in January 2006 had an associated HSA. The Commonwealth Fund/EBRI survey also stated that, of the roughly 10 million people enrolled in

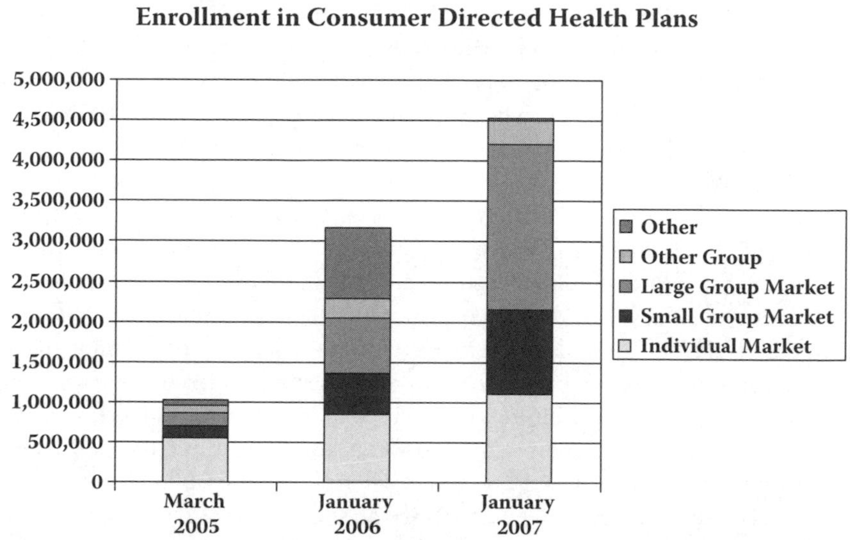

Enrollment in Consumer Directed Health Plans

Figure 3.3   *Source*: America's Health Insurance Plans—www.ahipresearch.org

some form of high-deductible health plan, only about 1.3 million were enrolled in a plan with an associated HRA or an HSA account.

There appear to be two reasons why not all high-deductible plans have accounts attached. The first is mechanical. Before people can be eligible for an HSA, they must first be enrolled in a qualifying high-deductible plan. The second reason is more fundamental, and to understand it we need to take a look at why people enroll in CDHPs or HDHPs. At least three different types of people seem to make use of these insurance vehicles:

■ *People for whom these policies are ideal*—individuals with higher incomes who are in good health. These people benefit from the lower monthly premiums often attached to the high-deductible plan. Since they have higher incomes, they generally do not face a serious economic risk if they run into health problems during the year—they have the means to cover the required out-of-pocket expenses. Their higher incomes also mean that they are capable of putting money into an HSA, and because of the higher tax bracket they are in, they will also reap the benefits of the tax-advantaged status these accounts enjoy.

■ *People who do not have a choice.* Some employers offer CDHP/HDHP as "full replacement" plans. In other words, the CDHP/HDHP is the only option offered. According to a survey conducted by the Center for Studying Health System Change, nearly 40% of workers enrolled in employer-sponsored CDHPs/HDHPs did not have a choice in the matter. The Commonwealth Fund/EBRI study stated that the percentage was even higher—54% for high-deductible plans and 42% for consumer directed plans. These individuals may or may not have a combination of health and income status that would allow them to benefit from the features these plans offer.

■ *People who purchase CDHPs/HDHPs primarily for the lower monthly premiums these plans often charge.* The Henry J. Kaiser Family Foundation's annual survey of employer health care benefits shows that in some cases, consumers can save 20% to 30% per month in premium costs by choosing a CDHP/HDHP. If consumers make this choice because they cannot afford the costs of more comprehensive coverage, then it is unlikely they would be able to fund the contributions to an HSA. How frequently does this occur? It is impossible to know with certainty, but when the Commonwealth Fund/EBRI survey asked consumers why they had enrolled in their particular plan, 49% of those in HDHPs and 53% of those in CDHPs mentioned the lower monthly premiums as one reason for their selection. This same survey asked individuals who were enrolled in a high-deductible plan that met the guidelines for HSA eligibility why they had not opened such an account. Among enrollees who had not opened accounts, 44% said they did not have the money, 20% said it was too much trouble to do so, and 19% said the tax benefits were not sufficiently attractive. The Center for Studying Health System Change survey mentioned above stated that, of workers who do have a choice of plans, only 19% select the consumer directed option, so this may not be a frequent occurrence. However, the low rate at which consumers volunteer for these plans when they do not have to is troubling for other reasons.

There is no good research on how the total number of CDHP/HDHP enrollees is divided among these various subtypes. The plans are still too new for definitive information. However, the potential for a "double whammy" effect of enrolling in such a plan due to lack of funds to afford anything else and then being hit with a significant medical problem requiring a good deal of out-of-pocket costs means that this could be a serious problem for those affected. As a result, more study and better analysis of this important question is required.

It is clear that more employers are offering such coverage. According to the Henry J. Kaiser Family Foundation, the percentage of all employers offering any sort of high-deductible health plan has risen from 4% in 2005 to 7% in 2006 and to 10% in 2007. However, the increase between 2006 and 2007 was not statistically meaningful. Consumer directed health plans are offered almost twice as frequently by larger firms as by smaller ones. Looking at actual enrollment versus other sorts of health insurance, though, shows a 5% share of the entire employer sponsored health insurance market for any form of consumer directed plan, statistically unchanged from the 4% share reported in 2006, the first year the Kaiser Family Foundation reported meaningful enrollment in these vehicles.

To help motivate consumers to move to the consumer directed option, a number of employers are making contributions to health savings accounts, offering HRAs, and/or are raising the monthly contribution required to purchase other forms of coverage. The 2007 Henry J. Kaiser Family Foundation Employer Benefits survey found that employers contributed about $900 to an HRA for an individual policy and $1,800 for a family policy. Employer contributions to HSAs were smaller—about $400 for individual plans and about $700 for family policies.

Effects on Health Care Costs, Utilization, and Quality

One thing that supporters and detractors of consumer directed health care generally do agree on is that these plans reduce short-term costs through decreased utilization of medical services. In the very early days of consumer directed health care, anecdotal reports from some early adopters claimed first year reductions of up to 20% in cost trends. For example, in March 2004, the head of human resources for Logan Aluminum gave testimony before Congress regarding his firm's initial experience with consumer directed care. He reported that the company had seen an 18.7% drop in total medical costs between 2002 and 2003. Considering that the firm had been experiencing 20% per annum health care cost increases, this result was striking. He further stated that there was no impact in employee's use of preventative health services or care needed for serious medical issues.

Owens Corning was another early adopter of consumer directed health care. In March 2005 representatives of the company provided results of their first year of experience with a consumer directed approach. They reported a 17% reduction in physician visits, a 42% drop in emergency room use, and 20% drop in prescription drug use. Unfortunately, they also reported declines in usage of preventative and screening services, even though these services were exempted from the deductible. At the time, Owens Corning was unable to say whether any of the reductions in utilization came from enrollees forgoing necessary medical services.

A more recent report was published by the major health insurer Cigna in October 2007, describing the firm's experience with its "Choice Fund" product. This report stated that cost trend growth in this CDHP plan was "less than half" that seen for HMOs and preferred provider organizations (PPOs). It further said

HDHP Consumption Of Medical Services

In the past 12 months, was there a time when, *because of cost,* you...

	General Public %	HDHP %	Difference %
Did not fill a prescription	21	27	-6
Had a specific medical problem but did not visit a doctor	32	38	-6
Did not receive a medical test, treatment or follow-up that was recommended by a doctor	23	29	-6
Took a medication less often than your doctor recommended	19	23	-4
Took a lower dose of a prescription medication than what your doctor recommended	12	17	-5

Figure 3.4 *Source*: Harris Interactive, Strategic Health Perspectives 2007

that out-of-pocket costs for members were similar and that the use of preventative services and medication compliance increased.

The Harris Interactive survey CDHP/HDHP also suggests that members of such plans use less care. While the Harris survey provides qualitative rather than quantitative information, the pattern it shows regarding use of services has been consistent for several years, and it shows a somewhat different and more troubling picture regarding how this utilization reduction is achieved. The details are shown in Figure 3.4.

In 2006 Harris Interactive looked at the question of whether consumer behavior was different when the plan had an HRA/HSA associated with it instead of simply a high-deductible plan. Surprisingly, consumers did not really behave differently with respect to reducing care even if they did have an available spending account. Bear in mind that the Harris survey did not tell us how much of the avoided care was "necessary" versus "unnecessary." As a result, it did not indicate whether or not the health of enrollees was damaged due to these reductions in the use of medical services.

The Henry J. Kaiser Family Foundation survey also supported the theory that CDHP plan enrollees reduce their use of care. Twenty-six percent of CDHP enrollees said they had not filled a prescription within the past year because of cost, compared to only 15% of the control group (people enrolled in more traditional health plans). Twenty-five percent of CDHP enrollees said they had skipped a recommended test or treatment. Twenty-three percent reported needing medical care and not getting it due to cost. Both these percentages were far higher than what was reported among members of the control group. Once again, though, the Kaiser Family Foundation survey was silent on whether there was actual medical harm done to these CDHP members as a result of their not receiving care.

The Commonwealth Fund/EBRI survey was a bit more equivocal. It said that there was less variation in the frequency with which CDHP/HDHP members used health services versus people enrolled in more traditional plans. There were two exceptions. People in HDHPs were more likely not to have visited a doctor within the past year, and people in both CDHPs and HDHPs were less likely to have received a diagnostic test of any kind in the past year. Both groups were also less likely to have been treated in an emergency room than their counterparts with traditional insurance. The survey made no comment on whether there were negative medical outcomes as a result of these behaviors.

An academic analysis of the early impact of consumer directed health care on costs was conducted by Melinda Buntin and her colleagues. It was published as a web exclusive by *Health Affairs* in October 2006. Their work was also summarized in "Research Highlights" published by RAND Health. These researchers confirmed that consumer directed health plans were associated with short-term reductions in both cost and utilization of services. They cited five separate reports of consumer directed health plan implementation. If such plans were put into effect with no accompanying account (either an HSA or an HRA), the savings ranged between 4% and 15%. If accounts were added to the basic high-deductible plan, savings dropped to 2.5% to 7.5%. The reduction was due to the tax-advantaged status of the accounts, which appeared to moderate the cost-containment incentives that a plain high-deductible plan offers. They went on to look at various categories of service use and found that the largest effect was as a more than 10% reduction in primary care office visits. Hospital admissions and hospital bed-days were also reduced, but to a much lesser extent.

In short, consumers who are faced with the increased cost-sharing burdens of high-deductible plans do use less health care, and as a result, total health care spending is reduced, at least for the short term. There does appear to be some disagreement about the amount of cost savings that occurs. The highest reported figures, if sustained over time, would represent a significant change in national spending. The lower end of the figures reported by Buntin and her colleagues would be far less important. What we do not know, and cannot know for some time yet is the *long-term* effect on costs and utilization. For those with long memories, there have been other solutions to health care's problems over the past several decades that produced equally dramatic results in the short term, only to run into problems trying to sustain their initial results. In fact, over the course of the past thirty-plus years, no intervention has been able to produce a meaningful and sustained reduction in the national health care spending trend. The pressures discussed in the previous chapter have eventually overwhelmed every attempt to contain them. Perhaps consumer directed health care will be the first to succeed, but history suggests caution in drawing conclusions at this point.

A question that will likely have a great bearing on the sustainability of current consumer directed health care products is their impact on quality. The early experience of passing financial risk to physician groups serves as a potentially cautionary tale. If consumers are somehow able to make effective judgments about what care they need and do not need—if they are able to seek out the former and avoid the latter—then there would be grounds for considerable optimism. Here, unfortunately, the picture is more mixed.

Buntin and her colleagues used that exact word—"mixed"—to describe CDHP's effect on medical quality. As we have seen from the RAND Health Insurance Experiment, consumer cost shifting is a very blunt instrument, producing reductions in nearly all forms of care, good and bad alike. Although a great number of consumer directed plans do exempt various forms of preventative care from patient cost sharing, it is not entirely clear how aware consumers are of that fact or how often they avail themselves of these services.

The Cigna report was probably the most encouraging information we have in this regard, but the more independent surveys conducted by Harris Interactive and the Henry J. Kaiser Family Foundation both reached very different conclusions.

The independent academic work from Buntin et al., showing that much of the reduction in health care utilization came from declines in primary care office visits, is potentially troubling. Since primary care is the point of first entry for our health care system and the place where many preventative services should be delivered, declines in utilization of these providers needs to be examined in more detail. The Harris Interactive survey is also a potential concern, because it reflects a multiyear comparison of the behavior of high-deductible plan enrollees versus individuals with more traditional insurance. Unfortunately, this research does not give any indicators of whether the care avoidance behavior applies to needed or unneeded care. The Harris Interactive SHP surveys also asked employers about their attitudes toward consumer directed health care. Roughly half of the respondents to the 2007 survey thought that consumer directed care would indeed cause consumers to forego necessary care—about the same percentage as thought these plans would cause consumers to spend more wisely on care. Admittedly, these questions reflect opinions rather than tangible results, but the comments are potentially instructive.

Other interesting data, while not specific to consumer directed health plans, do help speak to the effect of reducing utilization of health care resources on quality. In July 2007, Dana Goldman and his colleagues from RAND Health published a detailed analysis on the results of cost sharing on prescription drug consumption and on outcomes. As discussed in the previous chapter, the growth of "tiered" prescription drug plans has increased the out-of-pocket costs for medications borne by consumers. Because these programs have existed for the better part of a decade, Goldman and his collaborators went back to evaluate the academic literature on the effects they have had on consumer behavior. They reviewed over 900 articles and focused on over 100 where the data were of sufficient quality to permit a detailed analysis. What they concluded was that cost sharing did reduce consumption of prescription drugs. Treatment rates were lower, compliance with therapy regimens was lower, and discontinuation rates were higher. These effects occurred across all drug classes the researchers studied, and they concluded that a 10% increase in patient costs resulted in a 2% to 6% decline in prescription drug spending. Perhaps their most concerning finding was that for several important chronic diseases, this greater cost sharing was also associated with greater use of other medical services. If the conclusions from this research extend to other forms of health care, then we need to be paying far more attention to the effects that consumers' reductions in health care service consumption might have on their overall health a few years down the road.

Shopping Behavior

One of the most basic principles of consumer directed health care is that the increased cost sharing will force consumers to be good shoppers for health care services. Is there evidence that consumers in the current crop of consumer directed plans actually shop for their care? The answer appears to be a qualified "yes." Many of the various surveys issued by the insurers who offer such plans make this claim, but more objective confirmation can be found in data from the Harris Interactive survey. During early 2007, the firm asked members of the general public about various behaviors that represent various forms of shopping behavior and compared their responses to several consumer subsets, including those enrolled in high-deductible health plans. The results are shown in Figure 3.5.

What is striking about these findings is not that the high-deductible enrollees shopped more, but how little any of the groups engaged in *any* of the behaviors.

Results from the Henry J. Kaiser Family Foundation survey showed a similar result. Twelve percent of CDHP enrollees said they "almost always" asked about the price of a doctor's office visit before making an appointment. That compared to 6% for a control group of non-CDHP participants. The same survey showed that 23% of CDHP enrollees "almost always" asked about cheaper alternatives for recommended medical procedures compared to just 10% of the control group.

Shopping For Health Care

Thinking About Current/Most Recent Plan, in the Past 12 Months, Have You...?

	HDHP %	Public %	Seniors %	Boomers %
Paid more out-of-pocket to see a doctor outside of your plan	15	10	3	11
Challenged a decision regarding your own or a family member's care	18	11	6	11
Complained to your employer about a problem with your health plan	17	7	1	9
Paid more out-of-pocket to see a better doctor	17	11	6	11
Switched doctors to lower your out-of-pocket costs	8	4	1	4
Switched to a less expensive health plan	17	7	5	5
Switched to a more expensive health plan	8	6	2	6
Dropped your health coverage altogether	1	2	-	1
Talked to your doctor about your out-of-pocket costs for major diagnostic costs	19	9	5	8

Figure 3.5 *Source*: **Harris Interactive, Strategic Health Perspectives 2007**

Perhaps even more interesting is another question Harris Interactive asked of both the general public and high-deductible plan enrollees. This related to confidence in being able to obtain good value for money when purchasing various goods and services. The firm first queried respondents about their confidence in being able to shop effectively for several nonhealth care purchases. As Figure 3.6 shows, there was no significant confidence difference seen between the general public and HDHP enrollees for these decisions. However, when the questioning moved to ask about health care-related purchases of various sorts, the overall confidence of both groups dropped, and the high-deductible insurance plan enrollees exhibited larger losses of confidence than did members of the general public. These are differences were most pronounced for health care's "big-ticket" items, hospital services and insurance. There are a number of potential explanations for these findings. First, it is probably more difficult to actually make these sorts of decisions than to talk about doing so in abstract terms. Second, as we will see later on, there is a real lack of the sort of information that consumers really need. Finally, as we will also see, there are concerns about consumers' "health literacy," which speaks to their ability to interpret health care information and make effective decisions.

The Henry J. Kaiser Family Foundation survey showed similar results. Only 6% of CDHP enrollees surveyed strongly agreed that they felt comfortable negotiating price with physicians. Only 5% believed they could get a better deal on prices for medical services than could their insurance company, and only 4%

Consumer Confidence In Decision-Making Ability

When you consider purchasing the following products or services how confident are you in your ability to get the best value for your money?	% HDHP Confident	% General Public Confident
Clothing	48	47
Consumer Electronics	39	38
Tax Preparation	39	37
Autos	32	33
Dentists	27	26
Prescription Drugs	24	26
Hospital Services	15	20
Health Insurance	11	20

Figure 3.6 *Source*: **Harris Interactive, Strategic Health Perspectives 2007**

strongly agreed that they could do better than their insurance company when it came to obtaining prices for hospital services.

Consumer directed health plan members are not the only people who are facing significant out-of-pocket costs for health care. Most consumers in the United States are feeling increased health care-related financial pain in the form of increased copayments and deductibles, not to mention the rising number of uninsured. If we look beyond just those behaviors that can be directly attributed to the effects of consumer driven health plans, there are clear signs that more consumers are starting to shop around for health care.

Retail or "walk-in" clinics are a relatively recent phenomenon. They generally are found in retail pharmacy chains or very large retailers like Wal-Mart. These clinics are usually staffed by nurse practitioners and treat a variety of low-grade common acute health care problems like sore throats and earaches in children or strains and sprains in adults. They are open far more hours than the average physician's office, and no advance appointment is necessary. Prices are generally much cheaper than the full cost of a physician's office visit. Use of such clinics has been modest so far, but is growing. Harris Interactive conducted a survey on the use of these clinics as part of its 2007 Strategic Health Perspectives offering and found that only 7% of the general public had visited such clinics. However, usage appears set to grow, and experts expect the number of such clinics to grow in the coming years. Greater convenience and lower prices appear to be the main drivers of current and future use. While such clinics do not presently treat chronic illness, it is possible that they might begin doing so at some point in the future. This would almost certainly expand their appeal and their usage even further and faster.

Retail clinics are controversial in the medical community. At least one group—the American Academy of Pediatrics—has recommended that patients not seek care from them. The American Medical Association is calling for increased scrutiny of such clinics, and the American Academy of Family Practice has suggested some guidelines under which it would endorse their use. It is difficult to know how much of the concern from organized medicine is driven by worries about potential problems with patient care and how much is driven by concerns about the financial impact such clinics could have on physician incomes. There will almost certainly be more discussions about the role of such clinics in the coming years.

Consumer directed health care is certainly not the only factor driving the emergence, use, and expansion of retail clinics, but it would be hard to imagine that such clinics would not be an attractive option for enrollees, at least under some circumstances. We might expect to see other innovations in ambulatory care emerge from a combination of consumer driven health care and cost pressures facing consumers in general.

"Medical tourism" is a relatively new phrase in the health care dictionary. It refers to the practice of seeking medical care outside the borders of the United States. Some Europeans have used medical tourism as a way to avoid waiting for care at home, and medical tourism is already a multibillion dollar industry. In the past few years, more Americans have begun to consider it as an option. The potential cost savings for U.S. patients willing to travel abroad are considerable. According to a 2007 report on the topic prepared by the NCPA, heart bypass surgery in the United States is priced at about $210,000. Insurers receive a negotiated price of roughly $94,000. That same surgery would cast $20,000 in Singapore, $12,000 in Thailand, and just $10,000 in India. While this is the most dramatic difference seen among eight procedures NCPA reported on, savings of between 25% and 50% were common. Even after including the cost of airfare and lodging, the opportunity to save money is dramatic. While going to Asia for surgery might conjure up some unpleasant images of third-world conditions of medical quality and cleanliness, this is not necessarily the case. Some of the more prestigious institutions catering to foreigners seeking medical care are staffed by physicians trained in the West and are sometimes accredited by reputable bodies. A good deal of medical tourism happens closer to home, with Mexico and Latin America among the destinations for Americans looking for bargains. The NCPA estimated that 500,000 Americans sought medical care abroad during 2005. Another source projects that 750,000 Americans sought care abroad in 2007, with perhaps as many as 6 million doing so in 2010. There are already medical intermediaries such as Planet Hospital and MedRetreat that will assist Americans in finding care abroad. The NCPA estimated that, if 10% of the top 50 low-risk treatments were performed abroad, the United States could save a collective $1.4 billion annually.

Why are these procedures so much less expensive abroad than in the United States? The answer lies in the factors we discussed in Chapter 2. The most important of these is the difference in labor costs, especially the salaries of the physicians, nurses, and other support staff whose paychecks make up such a large component of health care costs all over the world.

As is the case with retail clinics, it is unlikely the consumer directed health care enrollees are entirely responsible for all the interest in medical tourism, but an enrollee confronted with the need for a nonemergency procedure would almost certainly have some degree of interest in exploring the possible cost savings to be had by going abroad. A January 2007 article in *Health Affairs* stated that, for savings of $10,000 or more, 38% of the uninsured and 25% of those with health insurance would travel outside the United States for care. There are reports that large employers are putting pressure on U.S. insurers to cover procedures performed abroad. In some places, Blue Cross Blue Shield is already selling policies that cover procedures performed abroad.

There are some signs of response from the U.S. health care system. A May 2007 article in *Forbes* magazine stated that one U.S. hospital, the Black Hills Surgery Center of Rapid City, South Dakota, was offering highly discounted knee replacement surgery. The Geisinger Health System of central Pennsylvania recently announced a "flat rate" for various forms of surgery that includes a 90-day follow-up period. While these rates are not necessarily discounted, they do provide some assurance for patients that their costs will not exceed a given amount.

Also like retail clinics, medical tourism is controversial. There are very limited legal remedies available to patients who experience problems, and for certain procedures the act of traveling itself could represent a challenge. However, given the very significant cost savings available, it seems likely that this approach to saving health care costs will continue to grow.

Consumer Satisfaction

While consumer directed health care's primary goal is to bring down the rate of growth in health care costs by forcing consumers to "self-ration" their own care, the long history of health care reform teaches us that no tactic to change how health care is delivered can last if consumers are not happy with it. As a result, it is very important to look at how enrollees in CDHPs and HDHPs feel about them and how satisfied they are this with this new form of health insurance.

One measure of satisfaction is which health plans consumers select when given a choice. We have already seen from the Henry J. Kaiser Family Foundation survey that relatively small numbers of patients voluntarily select a CDHP option when they have a choice. The Center for Studying Health System Change report that we have already briefly discussed said that a large percentage of patients in these new insurance plans did not have a choice.

The Henry J. Kaiser Family Foundation asked CDHP enrollees and the control group how likely they would be to switch health plans, given the opportunity to do so. Sixteen percent of CDHP enrollees said they were "very likely" to do so, and 34% responded "somewhat likely." This compared to 7% of the control group who said they were very likely to switch and 26% who said they were somewhat likely to do so. The same survey showed that, while 57% of CDHP enrollees would give their health plan a grade of A or B, that was lower than the 69% of individuals in the control group who gave that rating to their plan. The differences were much less between the two groups when asked about their ability to see a doctor when needed, but were much greater when the question addressed out-of-pocket spending.

The Harris Interactive survey questioned both CDHP/HDHP enrollees and members of the general public about satisfaction with particular aspects of care. For issues related to access, like the ability to see a doctor whenever needed, there were no differences between the two groups, and about 80% of both groups were either "very" or "somewhat" satisfied. Given that consumer directed health plans do not put any preapproval barriers between consumers and care, this is not particularly surprising. On questions related to happiness with insurance benefits and costs, the answers were quite different. Only 54% of CDHP/HDHP enrollees were satisfied with their health insurance benefits versus 75% of the general public. Only 44% of CDHP/HDHP enrollees said they were satisfied with their monthly insurance premiums versus 62% of the general public.

The Commonwealth Fund/EBRI survey also asked about satisfaction and got similar answer. While 76% of those with conventional insurance coverage said they were "extremely" or "very" satisfied with their plan," 57% of HDHP enrollees and 63% of CDHP enrollees gave the same response, and these differences were statistically significant. When the questions addressed out-of-pocket spending, the gaps between the two groups were dramatic. Forty-six percent of the control group were "extremely" or "very" satisfied while only 18% of HDHP and 20% of CDHP members felt the same way.

It is still probably too early to make a final call about whether consumers in high-deductible plans are truly satisfied with their insurance coverage. Not surprisingly, the cost issues appear to be the biggest negative. We will need more time and more evidence before being able to reach more definitive conclusions, but the early results from all three of our survey sources suggest there are some reasons for concern.

Issues Affecting Consumer Directed Health Care

The basic questions we have discussed are, like how many members, what is the effect on costs, do consumers shop, and how satisfied are they, give us a common base of understanding about today's CDHP/HDHP products. There are several somewhat more theoretical issues that we need to discuss in order to have a better grasp of the prospects for these insurance vehicles, and we will discuss these next.

Individual versus Group Insurance

Health insurance provided by employers or under government programs like Medicare and Medicaid is what is called group insurance. That means that the insurance is purchased for a large number of people at the same time by a single purchaser. There are a number of good reasons why this is the standard model for insurance coverage, and one of the most important is the potential for risk pooling. As we discussed earlier, risk pooling is important because it makes insurance affordable for people who actually need to consume health care. This is accomplished by using the premiums from relatively healthier enrollees to help pay for the services consumed by sicker enrollees. We have talked a bit about how concentrated health care spending is among a relatively small number of people, but it is difficult to understand the impact at a population level. In 2002, Scott Serota, who is the president and CEO of the BlueCross BlueShield Association, the nation's largest private health insurer, wrote an article in *Health Affairs* in which he described exactly how important this cross subsidy is. Obviously, health insurance costs were lower then, but the comparisons made in the article still apply. Assuming an annual insurance cost of $1,500 per person per year, a plan would need 22 enrollees who pay full premiums but collect no benefits of any kind to support one enrollee with ovarian cancer. For other, more costly diseases, the numbers get worse. To support one person who requires a kidney transplant, a plan would need 95 "zero-cost" enrollees. To support the costs of one premature infant, 193 zero-cost enrollees are needed.

Why is this relevant? Consumer directed health plans are far more likely to be individual rather than group policies. In fact, they are increasingly the only sort of coverage that people buying insurance outside the group market can obtain. This means that, for such people, the safety net of cross subsidies that exist with group coverage go away in a high-deductible environment. That is not the only potential problem with individual insurance versus group insurance.

If there is no cross subsidy to protect the insurance company (and the beneficiary), then the insurance company needs to take a much closer look at the medical background of the individual applying for the policy. The term of art for this in the insurance industry is "medical underwriting." It means that the insurer will take a detailed look at your present and past health before deciding whether or not to issue you a policy. Any number of things in your medical history that might seem innocuous can make you ineligible for coverage in the eyes of an insurer.

It is not just historical problems that matter. If a beneficiary develops health problems in a given year, in the current individual health insurance market, there is a reasonable chance that he or she will not be offered coverage in the next year. It is also more likely that your insurer will go back through your application to see if there is any way your policy can be canceled during the year in which your medical condition occurred. This is called "recission" in the insurance industry. In the fall of 2007, WellPoint, a major California-based health insurer was found to have paid bonuses to employees for canceling policies after the fact, a practice that is illegal in California.

When an insurer tries to avoid writing coverage for people who need it, or revokes coverage for those who encounter problems, it is simply trying to protect its financial health. Medical underwriting is not illegal, nor is denying coverage. The issue in the WellPoint case was not that the firm engaged in recission; it was that it paid employees bonuses for the practice. Insurers operate on a "for-profit" basis, and in the current U.S. market, they are simply following the rules of the game. The "fix" for this problem is not to point fingers at insurance companies, but rather to change their incentives. This is an issue we will return to in the final chapter of the book.

A closely related issue is "favorable selection." In plain English, this refers to the question of whether people who enroll in consumer directed health plans are healthier than average. At first glance, this would appear to make sense. If a consumers were relatively younger and in better health, they would seem to be more willing to enroll in a CHDP, believing that they were unlikely to be subjected to the out-of-pocket expenditures associated with such plans. The actual evidence on this subject is mixed at best. Harris Interactive found only a slight difference between enrollees in consumer directed plans versus those with more traditional insurance coverage with respect to age and health status. The Henry J. Kaiser Family Foundation's survey of CDHP enrollees reached a similar conclusion. Sixty-four percent of CDHP enrollees in this study said they were in excellent or very good health versus 52% of those in the control group. The Commonwealth

Fund/EBRI survey concluded that enrollees in CDHP/HDHP products were more likely to be single, young, and white. They were also less likely to suffer from a chronic disease.

Of course, a consumer who selects a health insurance plan is making a bet about his or her health in the future. CDHP enrollees are, in effect, wagering that they will not experience significant medical problems and will therefore benefit from the lower premium without suffering the penalty of the high deductible. The Congressional Budget Office conducted a comprehensive analysis of consumer directed health plans in December 2006 and pointed out that people cannot always be certain about their future medical costs. People with low expenses one year can be confronted with unexpectedly high expenses the next. In contrast, people who encounter high medical costs one year might well drop back to more normal spending in a subsequent year. Statisticians refer to this phenomenon as "regression to the mean."

If enrollees in consumer directed plans were actually healthier (and, therefore, less costly) than enrollees in other plans, this would mean that we might have the potential for a rerun of what occurred in the 1980s with the advent of the first generation of managed care. Before the coming of managed care, most Americans were in "indemnity" plans, which were basically places to which providers submitted bills and received payment. There was little management of their expenses. As managed care became more common, it attracted those who were relatively healthier than average. This meant that costs for those who required care and were still in indemnity insurance plans skyrocketed and led to what was called at the time a "death spiral." Eventually, indemnity insurance became so expensive that it essentially became extinct. Given the escalating costs of health insurance at the time, this may have been a good thing, but it happened largely by accident. We have discussed the importance of cross subsidies in keeping insurance affordable, so this is an area we will need to watch closely as CDHPs continue to evolve.

We have already seen that administrative costs represent a far higher proportion of U.S. health care costs than in most other developed nations. Reducing these costs would seem to be some of the "low-hanging fruit" for health care reform. Within the current U.S. system, administrative costs are different for different sort of policies. In its report "A Roadmap for Health Insurance Reform. Principles for Reform," the Commonwealth Fund noted that such costs represented between 25% and 40% of the premium dollar for individual policies versus 10% for employer group policies and 2% for Medicare. This is almost certainly due to the greater sales and marketing spending required for an insurer to reach individual consumers versus that required to speak with an employer who purchases coverage for thousands of people all at once. It will be interesting to see over the long term whether or not this increased burden of administrative

Availability Of Health Care Price Data

How easy or difficult would you say it is to get prices for each of the following? (NET Easy)	% CDHP	% General Public
Prescription medications	69	66
Office Visits (primary care doctors, specialists, etc.)	65	61
Outpatient hospital care (including emergency room/urgent care)	29	32
Inpatient hospital care	24	30
Lab or diagnostic testing	39	38

Figure 3.7 *Source*: **Harris Interactive, Strategic Health Perspectives 2007**

costs continues and what effect it might have in erasing some of the financial benefits and health care utilization reductions that CDHPs produce.

Access to Data

Nearly all advocates of consumer directed health care will say that the success of such an approach depends on consumers being able to access reliable information about cost and quality. What do we know about the availability of such information? Harris Interactive, the Henry J. Kaiser Family Foundation, and the Commonwealth Fund/EBRI work have all explored parts of this subject. Harris Interactive asked CDHP enrollees how easy or difficult it was to get pricing information for a number of common medical services and compared their answers to those of the general public. The results of the Harris Interactive survey are seen in Figure 3.7.

Given the effort health plans have put into developing formularies over the past few years, it is not too surprising to see that prescription medicines top the list of easy-to-get information. What is more striking is the apparent difficulties encountered by both members of the general public and consumer directed health plan enrollees in getting pricing data on U.S. health care's single biggest cost component, hospital care. It is also worth noting that, while 2007 was the first year in which this question was asked specifically of enrollees in consumer directed plans, it was asked of the general public in 2006. For every category of spending, fewer consumers said it was as easy to get information in 2007 as responded "yes" to this question in 2006. In some cases, there was a 20% drop in the number of "easy" responses between the two years. There is no specific explanation to account for this interesting finding. It is possible (but not certain) that more people went looking for such information in 2007 than in 2006 and did not really realize how difficult getting such information was until they tried to do so.

The Commonwealth Fund/EBRI survey reported that enrollees in conventional insurance were *more* likely than CDHP/HDHP enrollees to say that their plan provided cost or quality information. This survey also looked at information-seeking behavior from other sources, something a proportion of respondents to this survey tried to do—although interestingly, people in CDHPs/HDHPs were no more likely than those with conventional coverage to have done so. Those enrolled in CDHPs/HDHPs reported they were less likely to have found the information they were seeking.

The Henry J. Kaiser Family Foundation survey also asked consumer directed enrollees how easy or difficult it was to find trustworthy information on both price and quality for hospital and physician services. Forty-seven percent of respondents said it was either "very" or "somewhat" easy to get such information on quality. With respect to pricing data, respondents were not as bullish. Thirty-six percent of the CDHP enrollees said it was "very" or "somewhat" easy to get this information for physician services, and this number dropped to 33% for hospitals pricing.

It is intriguing that respondents in the Henry J. Kaiser Family Foundation survey found quality information easier to obtain than cost information. In general, the quality information is provided by health plans rather than physicians or hospitals and is largely extracted from the claims information they accumulate in the process of paying bills. Most physicians take issue with the use of this data as a sole determinant of quality measurement. Several plans have been providing consumers with physician ratings largely derived from claims information, and this was the topic of a letter from the New York Attorney General to some of the nation's largest health insurers. In October 2007, an agreement was reached between the New York Attorney General and at least one of the insurers, in which the insurer agreed to separate its ratings and to contribute to an independent organization that would work to better present this data.

It is clear that consumers, whether they are in high-deductible plans or more traditional insurance plans do not have access to all the information they need to make decisions and that some of the information that is available is controversial. A great deal more work will be needed to address this fundamental challenge.

The question we need to ask is, "how fair it is to ask consumers to make decisions about care today when we have not yet provided them with the required information to do so intelligently?" There are two sides to this debate. Consumer advocates claim that pressure from consumers will be a major factor in driving the availability of better data and will point to other industries where this has been the case. People on the other side of the debate claim that providers have significant power over how health care is delivered and what information about that care gets collected. Since many providers do not have electronic systems to capture or share this sort of data, it is very difficult to find. This is another one of those questions that require you to make up your own mind. Before doing so, though, it is helpful to look at two closely related questions that we will consider next.

Consumer Health Literacy

It is very hard to be a master contractor if you cannot read blueprints. One of the fundamental tenets of consumer directed health care is that patients are both willing and able to be the primary decision makers regarding their own care. There are certainly consumers who can do both, although the story that I used to open this chapter suggests that it may not be as easy as it sounds, even for people who are relatively sophisticated about health care issues. There is an old saying in marketing that goes, "you are not your own target market." What that means is that you should not necessarily assume your abilities or interests are representative of the people you are trying to sell something to. That is especially true in health care, where the policy elites who are often PhDs in one field or another have considerable influence over what sorts of new programs the rest of us will see in the future.

There is a large amount of data available on education levels and reading comprehension in the United States, and when this information is matched up against the sorts of communications common in health care, we can see the potential for problems. According to the U.S. Census Bureau, there are about 226.6 million adults in the United States—defined as people aged 18 or more. While about half of them have some education beyond high school, 16% are high school dropouts, and the remaining third are high school graduates. For the population aged 18 to 24, nearly 48% have some college. Older adults tend to have somewhat lower educational levels than younger ones.

Education does not always translate into reading ability. Many health care communications are written at a grade level well beyond the reading comprehension level of typical adults. Several studies have shown that, on average, American adults read at about the sixth-grade level, and that fully 20% of the U.S. adult population is functionally illiterate. For some subsets of the population, the percentage is higher. Groups such as American Academy of Family Physicians and the Joint Commission on Accreditation of Healthcare Organizations have recommended that health care communications be targeted at somewhere between the fifth- and the eighth-grade level. Unfortunately, a 2002 survey of health-related Web sites found that most were targeted at the eleventh-grade level or higher. The problem extends to written materials as well.

Roughly half of all patients do not understand how to take medications on an empty stomach, about a quarter do not know when their next medical appointment is scheduled, and almost 60% do not understand the standard informed consent form that most providers require patients to sign before proceeding with treatment. A 1993 survey found that the literacy problem was more acute among health care's regular users. Three-fourths of American adults with chronic disease scored in the lowest two literacy levels.

More recent reports continue to show that health literacy is a serious challenge in the United States today. In 2004, the Institute of Medicine concluded that 90 million adults, close to *one half* the adult population, have difficulty understanding basic health care information, and that these individuals had a higher rates of hospitalizations and emergency room use. In October 2007, a study done by Northwestern University found that 40% of patients taking blood pressure medications were unable to accurately remember which drugs they were taking. This number jumped to 60% among adults with low health literacy. A July 2007 report on another survey from the same university found that one-fourth of elderly patients were considered "medically illiterate," and that people who had difficulty comprehending medical information were more likely to die earlier than those whose reading and comprehension abilities were higher. An October 2007 survey by Fidelity Investments mentioned previously found that this problem is not limited to medical terminology—it extends to benefits terminology as well, with only one in seven workers having a strong understanding of key terms.

There is another piece of this puzzle. When most people think about literacy, they think about words. Health care is also about numbers—lots and lots of numbers. As a result, math skills also matter a great deal when we talk about the ability to comprehend and use health information. The problem here might actually be worse. Researchers from the University of Oregon looked at this question in an article published in the May/June 2007 issue of *Health Affairs*. According to their work, almost half the general public has problems with everyday math-oriented tasks like figuring out how much of a discount they are getting in a sale, or calculating the cost per ounce from those grocery store labels we all see every time we go food shopping. Since things such as the likelihood of having an adverse event from a particular treatment, the health risks associated with certain behaviors, or the quality ratings for doctors and hospitals are all expressed primarily with numbers, this is potentially a serious concern.

What makes all this even more important is the relative complexity of current consumer directed health care plans. The Henry J. Kaiser Family Foundation survey found that enrollees in CDHPs were less likely to agree that their health plan was easy to understand. The Commonwealth Fund/EBRI survey found that only 46% of those in HDHP and 45% of those in CDHPs said their plan was easy to understand versus 65% with conventional coverage. In essence, it appears that current CDHPs/HDHPs make it harder, rather than easier for people to understand their policies. Given the across-the-board challenges with health literacy in the United States, this is also a cause for potential concern.

Decision Making

We have looked at the availability of information and consumers' ability to make sense of it. Let us tie the two together by looking at three questions:

- Are consumers aware that information exists?
- Have they looked at it?
- How much decision-making authority do consumers actually want?

First, are consumers aware that information is available? The Henry J. Kaiser Family Foundation survey asked this question and found that about two-thirds of both CDHP enrollees and the control group said that their health plan had a Web site that provided health care information. We have already briefly discussed the finding from the Commonwealth Fund/EBRI survey that showed CDHP/HDHP enrollees were less likely to report that their plan offered such data.

All three surveys asked whether or not consumers had looked at the available data. The Henry J Kaiser Family Foundation survey data showed that less than 10% of either CDHP enrollees or the control group had done so. The Commonwealth Fund/EBRI survey showed that fewer CDHP/HDHP enrollees had attempted to use such information than those with conventional coverage. The Harris Interactive survey was somewhat more optimistic and looked at the issue by asking consumers about specific data elements relating to both price and quality information for physicians, hospitals, pharmaceuticals, as well as physician and hospital satisfaction scores. Enrollees in consumer directed plans were somewhat more likely to have reviewed this data than were members of the general public. Both groups were much more likely to have looked at data related to prescription drugs than information about doctors or hospitals. Given the proportion of drug costs paid for out-of-pocket, this probably is not too surprising, but hospitals and doctors represent a far greater percentage of the country's total health care bill, so there is clearly room for improvement.

A June 2006 study on consumer decision support tools conducted by the California Health Care Foundation pointed out that a number of researchers have reported that the available information has not yet had a great deal of impact on consumer decision making. This may be due to consumer literacy issues, lack of the data consumers really need, or some other factor, but it is clearly a potential cause for concern.

For the first time in 2007, Harris Interactive asked both members of the general public and enrollees in consumer directed plans what sort of decision-making role they preferred. There were three choices available: consumer led, provider led, and shared (i.e., doctor and patient decide together). There were surprisingly few differences between the two groups. Only about a quarter wanted to take the lead, and less than 10% wanted the provider to take the lead. The balance wanted to share decision making equally with their health care provider.

In a very insightful article on medical decision making from the Hastings Center entitled "How Do Patients Know?" Rebecca Kulka discussed the strengths and weaknesses that doctors and patients bring to this important process. The article reviewed some of the accepted wisdom in the field. It is widely assumed that doctors are in the position of being better able to judge the technical merits of any particular medical procedure, while patients bring an ethical framework—they know what seems right or wrong for them. Both perspectives are necessary to reach satisfying conclusions. The article points out that often it is not quite that simple. Generally patients do not have to make medical decisions every day, while it is a physician's stock and trade. Therefore, physicians can bring a perspective on what other people in similar situations have done. There are complex values-related issues wrapped around most medical decisions, and the experience of physicians can be a real help for patients, especially those who are in difficult situations. Even if we have challenges with specific cost/quality information, there is a great deal of general information available about health care these days, thanks largely to the Internet. Those consumers who choose to look for such content will have little trouble finding data from all sorts of places. The problem is that this process can feel like drinking from the proverbial fire hose, and there is no easy way for patients to determine which information is trustworthy and which is not. Therefore, what most patients need to do after such an information gathering trip is to sit down with a physician who can help them sort it all out.

There is a final important aspect to the entire issue of information provision and consumer decision making, and that is legal liability. This is a gray area at present, and as CHDPs evolve, the courts will almost certainly play a role in that evolution. As we saw above, at least one state has gotten involved in the question of the accuracy and source of information provided to patients. An article by Peter Jacobson and Michael Turik published in the May/June 2007 issue of *Health Affairs* dealt with a number of the areas where the law is still very unclear in this space.

Perhaps the most fundamental question this article poses is who has the ultimate responsibility for ensuring that information provided to consumers is accurate and timely? In the traditional world of medicine as we know it, most of that burden fell on the shoulders of physicians. Physicians have generally been required to provide the same standard of care to all patients without considering their ability to pay. The informed consent providers obtain from patients generally covers the potential medical risks and benefits of therapy, not cost tradeoff issues. The Employee Retirement Income Security Act (ERISA) law that we discussed briefly in Chapter 1 provides a great deal of legal cover for employers and some for managed care as well. In the world that supporters of consumer directed health care would like to see, the patient takes the final responsibility for choosing his or her level of care based on economic and clinical considerations. Since patients do not have formal medical training, they need to rely on external information to make these decisions. When insurers offer decision-making tools to consumers, are they now held to a higher standard for accuracy and completeness? Will physicians, who are already pressed for time, be required to go through not just the clinical consequences of care decisions, but the economic ones as well? Finally, where will courts come down on a host of questions relating to patient competence to make these decisions?

None of this means that we cannot see evolution in the legal system or changes in accountability for care decisions, but it does mean that we are likely to see a good deal of litigation over the next several years, a lot of which will take us into some fundamental questions of fairness and health policy. Since these discussions will take us into new areas, it is important for all of us to think about them and be prepared to make our views known one way or the other.

When we combine the patchy information, the problems with consumer health literacy, the consumer need for physician help in making good medical decisions, consumer's preference for shared decision making, and the potential for significant legal issues, it is clear that a large number of consumers simply are not in the position to be the captain of their own ship when it comes to health care, at least not now. Expecting them to do so, or expecting that pressure from them will quickly reform the delivery system probably qualifies as overoptimistic. However, it is also clear that the era of patients passively doing whatever they are told by providers is also at an end. If we want health care to be truly consumer directed, we will need to think about additional ways to help patients, and we will discuss some of the options in the final chapter of the book.

Financial and Administrative Issues

Increased cost shifting to consumers is supposed to be the primary motivator of behavior change in consumer directed health care. So far, we have seen evidence that points out places where this new empowerment of consumers has had some

Consumer Concerns About Health Care Coverage And Costs

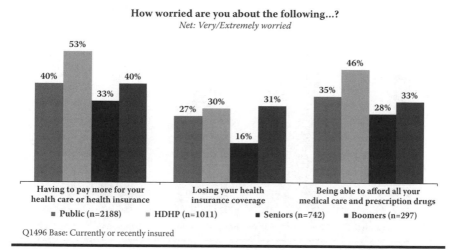

How worried are you about the following...?
Net: Very/Extremely worried

| Having to pay more for your health care or health insurance | Losing your health insurance coverage | Being able to afford all your medical care and prescription drugs |

■ Public (n=2188) ■ HDHP (n=1011) ■ Seniors (n=742) ■ Boomers (n=297)

Q1496 Base: Currently or recently insured

Figure 3.8 *Source*: **Harris Interactive, Strategic Health Perspectives 2007**

positive effects and places where the result has not been as favorable. There is real money involved in this equation, and we also need to take a look at the impact of consumer directed health care's cost requirements on consumers.

First, how much difference does being enrolled in a consumer directed plan make? Harris Interactive asked both members of the general public and CDHP enrollees how much they spent out of pocket on health care over the preceding twelve months. The average for the general public was a bit less than $1,500, while CDHP enrollees spent almost $2,400 annually—almost a 60% difference and almost 2% of the entire median household income in the United States.

Does this amount make a difference in consumers' perceptions of their financial security? Both Harris Interactive and the Kaiser Family Foundation survey posed questions that address this issue. Both surveys showed that CDHP enrollees felt significantly more financially exposed. By roughly a 2:1 ratio CDHP enrollees participating in the Kaiser survey felt less protected by their plan than did the control group. The Harris Interactive survey asked several subsets of consumers about their concerns regarding health care costs and coverage. The responses are shown in Figure 3.8.

The financial aspects of care are clearly more worrying to those in consumer directed, high-deductible plans than other consumer groups.

Harris Interactive further asked segments of the public how large a financial burden they faced from health care costs. As shown in Figure 3.9, those in

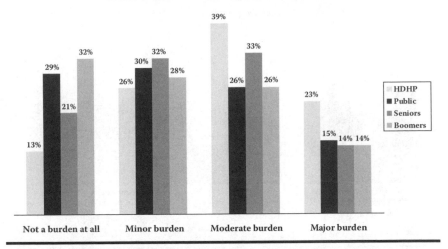

HDHP Consumers Feel a Larger Financial Burden of the Costs of Their Medical Care

Figure 3.9 *Source*: **Harris Interactive, Strategic Health Perspectives 2007**

CDHPs/HDHPs clearly believe that they face a larger challenge than do other segments of consumers.

The Commonwealth Fund has led the way in describing a new phenomenon—underinsurance. This word refers to individuals who are technically insured but have such high out-of-pocket burdens that they delay or defer care due to cost concerns. Interestingly, the presence or absence of an account generally did not make much of a difference in consumers' happiness with these plans. As we have already seen, large numbers of enrollees in HSA-eligible high-deductible plans said they did not have enough money to open an account, found it too much trouble to do so, or said that the tax benefits were not sufficiently attractive.

This survey also asked those with accounts how much money they rolled over from one year to the next. Twenty-three percent of those with accounts and thirty-five percent of those with a health problem rolled nothing over. About 20% of respondents were able to roll over $1,000 or more, with most of the remainder of respondents carrying balances of less than $1,000 from one year to the next. About 20% of people did not know whether they carried a balance over from one year to the next.

Enrollees in the both high-deductible and consumer directed plans were also asked about their total out-of-pocket spending as a percentage of their household income. About half of all those in both groups said they spent 5% or more of their household income on health care. Over 60% of people with household incomes of less than $50,000 spent at least 5% of their income on health care.

These figures do not address the question of whether or not it is appropriate to ask people to spend this much of their income on health care, but it is clear that, whether the consumer directed plan does or does not include a spending account, these vehicles impose a much heavier financial burden on enrollees than does traditional insurance.

Medical costs are now an important economic issue for consumers. An October 2006 poll conducted by *USA Today* and the Henry J. Kaiser Family Foundation found that one in four Americans were having trouble paying their medical bills, and 69% of these had insurance. One 2005 study from Harvard University published in *Health Affairs* found that one in four personal bankruptcies in the United States was due to health care costs, and that half had a significant medical component. It is important to note that these studies looked at health care costs in general, not just consumer directed plans, but the increased cost requirements of these plans almost certainly ensure that they will contribute to this problem. In fact, the Harvard study pointed out that a number of the families surveyed ran into financial difficulties at debt levels well below the out-of-pocket spending caps currently imposed on high-deductible plans. The authors of the Harvard study pointed out that a bankruptcy is more common among middle class families than the chronically poor, because the poor generally do not have the opportunity to incur the sort of debt levels that are available to people with higher incomes and more assets. In recent years, a number of news stories have suggested that average American households may be only one major illness away from bankruptcy.

There is another side to the increased consumer financial burden of CDHPs/HDHPs, and that is their effects on provider payments. According to one consulting report, providers normally write off about 5% of billings as bad debt. That number is expected to rise by 60%, to 8% of total billings, as CDHPs become more common. Given the relatively low posttax profit margins earned by most providers, even small changes could make a significant difference to their financial health. Three-quarters of physicians surveyed by Harris Interactive agreed that consumer directed/high-deductible plans would lead to greater problems with collecting patient's fees and bad debts. Fifty-seven percent of all physicians surveyed said the overall effect of such plans would be negative for patients, and fifty-two percent said such plans would be negative for themselves.

To avoid these problems, providers have to retool their entire approach to collecting payments. Beyond the obvious strain this puts on the doctor–patient relationship, there are also considerable administrative questions. How can a provider know whether or not a particular patient has met his/her annual deductible? Unless the insurer has a relatively sophisticated system in place and patients are diligent about reporting their out-of-pocket spending during the time when they receive no financial assistance, this can become a very significant problem.

Several major banks are beginning to roll out health-care-specific debit cards tied to HSAs or HRAs, and these will eventually help with consumers who have an account associated with their high-deductible health plan. This is a new and potentially very profitable line of business for these institutions and explains why they are so enthusiastic about consumer directed health care. Unfortunately, as we have seen, the vast majority of HDHPs do not have such associated accounts.

Employers are increasingly aware of the administrative challenges associated with consumer directed health plans. The Harris Interactive Strategic Health Perspectives survey asked in both 2006 and 2007 about the difficulties of administering such plans. While 77% of employers surveyed in 2006 thought such plans were either very easy or somewhat easy to administer, only 52% thought so in 2007. While there are some fixes for these administrative challenges, they are still not widely available, and this is yet another place where we are going to need to do some work to make these plans easier to operate.

What Sort of Health Insurance Plans Do Consumers Want?

One key issue in evaluating the current crop of CDHPs is to better understand what sort of health insurance consumers would design, given the opportunity to do so. A small project conducted for California Health Care Foundation by Sacramento Healthcare Decisions, the results of which were published in June 2007, gave some insight into that question. Uninsured Californians were asked to allocate a fixed amount of resources to a relatively broad number of choices for medical services that could be insured and to develop cost-sharing requirements to access those services. In other words, this project mimicked real-world conditions where the funds available for health care are limited and will not cover all the care anyone could possibly want.

While participants did not generally select "first-dollar" coverage for most services, neither did they select the sort of very high cost-sharing requirements that are part of current consumer directed plans. They also did not generally value the unlimited choice that is the hallmark of current CDHPs, but instead were willing to trade a degree of choice among available physicians for lower out-of-pocket costs. Respondents also placed a higher value on frequently used services and were willing to forgo a degree of coverage for some very expensive but infrequently used services to be able to afford such coverage. Finally, respondents were interested in tailored cost sharing. They seemed to believe that out-of-pocket expenditure for health care should vary by the amount of household income and also by whether or not the medical problem was caused by something the patient might have been able to prevent.

The sample size (121) in this project was limited, so its results can hardly be called definitive, but the insights are interesting. The October 2007 survey conducted by Fidelity Investments that we mentioned briefly before also provided some additional support for these conclusions. Seventy-four percent of workers in this study who did not currently have a CDHP expressed no interest in enrolling in one. This was true even for workers who stated that the monthly cost of premiums was the primary factor in deciding which health plan to select.

There certainly is some good news for advocates of CDHPs in the Sacramento research, because the respondents did take a stand for a degree of individual accountability for behavior, as demonstrated by their willingness to penalize individuals whose own decisions had brought on their medical problems. However, the current consumer directed plans do not seem to match up well with what average consumers seem to want, and this may help explain why relatively few consumers voluntarily choose one of the current consumer directed health plans when given a choice.

The current CDHP situation has some potential parallels to the managed-care "revolution" of late 1980s and early 1990s. Employers were confronted with rapidly escalating health care costs and began to force their employees into forms of managed care with which those employees were not comfortable. While this approach worked for a while, by the mid-1990s the United States was in the midst of a full-scale "managed-care backlash." This led to something of an overreaction on the part of employers and insurers. For a while there was little effort to manage the costs of care, and our current situation was a direct result of that. If the past has any power to predict the future, the same sort of thing *might* happen with consumer directed health care if consumers are forced into insurance plans that do not fit their needs. Clearly, we require more research with average consumers to determine exactly what they would like and what tradeoffs they are willing to make. That would help to ensure that the next iteration of consumer directed health care actually meets the needs of consumers.

Summary

This has been a long chapter, and we have covered a lot of ground. Let us summarize what we know about consumer directed health care today, and what we have discussed about some of the potential issues associated with this innovative way of offering health insurance. First, in many ways, consumer directed health care is a response to the managed-care backlash of the 1990s. A lot of the thinking that shaped them came from some (but not all) of the findings of the RAND Health Insurance Experiment of the 1980s. These vehicles evolved over time and were generally a response from the politically conservative segment of American society, which was attempting to find a more market-based and patient-centered solution to the problems of health care cost escalation. A number of elements, including high-deductible insurance plans and tax-advantaged savings accounts came together over a number of years, culminating with several provisions of the 2003 MMA. A number of very influential stakeholders have found aspects of consumer directed health care to be, initially, very appealing.

Enrollment in these plans has grown off a very small base, and they now have about 4.5 million participants. As of 2006, though, only a relatively small percentage of enrollees in the high-deductible component of these plans also had an accompanying tax-advantaged savings account.

Consumer directed health plans do appear to be effective at reducing short-term cost growth, and practically every report suggests these vehicles do generate some immediate reduction in utilization. While a few of the pioneers suggested they had seen savings in the 20% range, later reports indicate that savings in the 5% to 15% range are likely. What we do not know, what we cannot know at this point, is whether nor not these savings are a one-time event or will be sustainable over time.

One of the reasons there is a concern about the sustainability of the short-term savings is the controversy about how such plans generate savings. There is no definitive information regarding the effects of consumer directed health care on medical quality, but based on a number of reports, there is reason to suspect that consumers enrolled in these vehicles cut back on both necessary and unnecessary care in roughly equal proportions. It will be some time before we have definitive answers on what this means with respect to patient outcomes. Longer-term evidence gathered from studying the effects of cost shifting for prescription drugs suggests that we have cause to be concerned.

Consumer directed plans also seem to be producing some shopping behavior among enrollees, although not yet at anything like the levels supporters would like. One favorable sign is the emergence of some new methods of delivering care, such as retail clinics and medical tourism. While these cannot be directly attributed to consumer directed health care, the increased patient cost sharing that is happening across the insurance spectrum is almost certainly responsible, and since consumer directed plans have the largest cost-sharing requirements of all, it is likely they are playing some role in helping to spur patient interest in these alternative delivery tools.

If we are serious about making health care insurance an individual rather than a group market, as many advocates of consumer directed health care suggest, we will need to address some potentially tricky questions about how to make these plans affordable for people who actually need medical care. Cross subsidies are a fact of life in all forms of insurance, and while this is not a big problem in large risk pools such as those created when a major employer offers group coverage, it could be a very significant challenge if all Americans were to purchase their own coverage.

The biggest issue facing consumer driven health care is probably the consumer himself or herself. Consumer driven health care presumes that people will have good information on health care cost and quality readily accessible, that they will access it, that they will be able to understand it, and that they will be capable of making good decisions after they have done so. There are very legitimate questions about all of these, and fixing the underlying problems is not likely to be either quick or cheap.

Another big potential challenge for consumer directed health care is the financial strain that health care costs in general can place on an average American family. People in consumer directed plans spend more out-of-pocket on their care than people with more traditional coverage. That certainly has the potential to lead to serious financial problems, although that is probably not a regular occurrence.

The consumer's financial exposure leads to some problems for providers as well. Bad debt in medicine is on the rise, and given the relatively low posttax profit margins for doctors and hospitals, this has the potential to be a growing problem for providers. High-deductible plans create administrative headaches for physicians and hospitals in sorting out whether a patient in a consumer directed plan is personally liable for a particular expense or has reached the cap and is now eligible for third-party reimbursement. Banks and credit card companies can help out with some fixes for the later problem, but those fixes will work better if consumers have an account associated with their high-deductible plan, and that is not common today.

Perhaps all these issues combine to help explain why consumer directed plans might not necessarily line up particularly well with what consumers actually want in health insurance. This is far from definitive, and the evidence is still pretty limited. However, the history of health care innovations that do not fit consumers' needs (such as the first generation of managed-care plans) suggests we need to pay careful attention to the issue. What we do know is that several indications seem to suggest that satisfaction with these plans is somewhat lower than with conventional insurance.

We probably have to give the current crop of consumer directed health plans a mixed grade. They have produced some beneficial effects, but there are problems as well. Depending on where you stand on some of the bigger policy questions we have been raising throughout the book, you may see the glass as either half-full or half-empty.

We tend to go through a fairly predictable cycle with respect to innovative ideas in health care. These ideas usually burst on the scene with a great deal of buzz from their enthusiastic supporters. Since we recognize we have problems in health care, we tend to be willing to give any idea that sounds at least reasonably plausible a try. The first version of any idea is never perfect, so when we put the innovation into place, we get a reality shock when we encounter the inevitable problems. When the problems become apparent, there is a tendency to overreact and throw the baby out with the bathwater. Finally, we figure out that there are some good points about the idea, and we wind up incorporating them and move on to the next hot concept. This is called the "hype cycle." The term was coined by Gartner Inc., a major IT consulting firm and was originally applied to innovations in computing. Unfortunately, it works just about as well in health care, and it often means we spend too much time assimilating the really beneficial concepts contained in innovative new ideas.

The problems we are now facing in U.S. health care do not allow us the luxury of repeating the past, and we have got too much at stake as a society not to take as much as we can from every innovation and to do so as fast as we can. So let us take a slogan from one of the last big bipartisan things we did as a country—welfare reform. If you remember that time, you may also remember the phrase "mend it, do not end it." That worked out pretty well, so let us spend the last of our time together seeing if we can do the same for consumer directed health care.

Chapter 4

Prescription for the Future

So far, my objective with this book has been to inform, not to offer a particular point of view. However, as we saw in the last chapter there are some critical issues with the current-generation consumer directed health plans (CDHPs) that do not appear to be self-correcting in the short-to-intermediate term. If these are not addressed they could be fatal flaws and could lead consumer directed health care down the well-worn path of failure that has been the fate of so many innovative ideas in U.S. health care. In this chapter, we will match what we learned in Chapter 2 about the drivers of our health care costs with what Chapter 3 showed us about the strengths and weaknesses of "version one" of consumer directed health care. Since innovations in health care need to evolve, this final chapter will offer a perspective on what we are going to need to make "version two" of consumer directed health care a long-lasting and effective part of U.S. health care reform.

First, let me start with some general advice. As you have seen throughout this book, health care is complex. The way we got to where we are is a series of accidents, temporary fixes all bolted together with a lack of any sort of strategic direction. The present U.S. health care system took more than half a century to evolve, and there are a lot of moving parts that will need to be aligned if we are to shift to a more sustainable place. Given the funding "crunch" that appears almost certain to hit us over the next several decades, it is important that we get serious about health care sooner rather than later. Because our problem is becoming more urgent by the day, it is tempting to reach for "quick fixes," especially when they come shrink-wrapped in a particular political ideology. Both the political left and the political right have their versions of the "truth" for health care, and both are badly flawed.

Folks from the left will claim that other countries do a better job of controlling health care costs than does the United States, and that health care in many of these countries is "free." As we have seen, while there is some truth in the first half of that statement, the second is simply wrong. As long as physicians, nurses, pharmacists, research scientists, and the myriad of other folks who make a health care system operate need to feed their families, health care will never be "free." Patients may not be paying large amounts of money out-of-pocket for their health care, but those costs have to go somewhere. Quite often, where they go is into tax rates that are considerably higher than what we have become accustomed to in the United States over the past several decades. The United States has had tax rates that were much higher, especially for the top income brackets, than we see today. While we could make a collective decision to use taxation as a larger proportion of the U.S. health care system's funding base and go back to tax rates of fifty or sixty years ago, that would not make health care free; it would just change the distribution of expenses to people who pay relatively higher tax rates.

On the other hand, folks from the political right will say that only by turning the health care system over to individual consumers can we avoid a big central bureaucracy and prevent health care rationing. It is true that other countries generally have a more centralized management structure than we do in the United States, and many Americans seem to be almost genetically more opposed to the idea of a larger governmental footprint in health care than are people in Europe and Japan. However, most of those countries offer as much choice of physicians as we enjoy in the United States. It is also completely false that a consumer-centered health care system will not ration care—it will just do so in a different way. As we have seen throughout this book, demand for health care exceeds its supply everywhere and is likely to do so for the indefinite future. As a result, there *has* to be rationing of some sort. The rationing in a consumer-centered system is accomplished by pricing health care beyond the economic reach of some number of citizens. For most people, there is not much difference between this and having to wait to receive services or having limits on the technology available to restore or maintain their health. The reason proponents of "version one" consumer directed health plans do not see it that way is because, generally speaking, they belong to higher income brackets and have enough disposable income that the economic rationing of current CDHPs will not affect them.

We also have another disagreement between our political poles. Democrats tend to worry more about coverage and the high number of uninsured Americans.

Republicans are more focused on the costs of care. There is much less of a difference here than meets the eye, because these two issues are very closely linked. As we saw in Chapter 1, U.S. health care costs are high and are rising much faster than other costs in our economy. This clearly creates financial pain for people who have insurance coverage as their copayments increase. It also causes more employers to drop insurance coverage as the price of buying coverage outstrips the overall value of workers to a particular business. We will not be able to solve the uninsurance problem until we solve the cost problem, because any program to extend coverage to more people will be overwhelmed by escalating costs. As we will see a bit later in this chapter, though, ensuring that all Americans have health coverage will also help to address the cost problem. This is just one example of how both political poles could benefit by collaborating to achieve their mutual goals.

To some extent, "version one" of consumer directed health care looks a bit like a quick fix from the ideological right. As we have seen, while the initial incarnation of these vehicles does help with the short-term health care cost trend growth, it suffers from a number of other problems. However, this does not mean that the concept of consumer engagement in health is somehow fatally flawed. Quite the contrary—we must find a way to make consumers a more active part of the health care system. The idea of engaging consumers is the first truly novel concept to appear on the U.S. health care policy landscape in more than two decades. However, we need to recognize that there is no magic about handing the current troubles of the U.S. health care system off to consumers and expecting them to succeed where others have failed. Rather, we probably need to do some serious repair work to the infrastructure to address the real causes of health care cost growth in the United States. Then we can ask more from consumers with some real hope of success. Finally, it is helpful to recognize that a consumer *centered* health care system is not necessarily the same thing as a consumer *financed* health care system. We absolutely need to have the former, but the later probably is not realistic.

One further failing that is common to the quick fixes of both the left and the right is how they treat the health care delivery system. The single-payer solution of the political left generally accepts the delivery system "as is" and mostly transfers the burden of paying for it from the private sector to the public sector. The fully "market-driven" approach from the political right solves the wrong problem. As we saw in Chapter 2, the reasons that the U.S. health care system costs so much have little to do the "moral hazard" argument, "overinsurance," or consumer-induced demand. They relate far more to questions of lack of care coordination, input prices (incomes), demand induced by providers triggered by a combination of perverse incentives and information asymmetry, and ready provider access to technology. George Halvorson is the chairman and chief executive of the

Kaiser Foundation Health Plan and Kaiser Foundation Hospitals. He is also one of the most thoughtful people in health care. He speaks and writes frequently on health policy issues and, during 2007, he made the comment that health care reform ought to be about health care rather than health care *finance*. He has a point. As we saw in Chapter 1, we do not get particularly good value for the enormous amounts of money we pour into our health care system. Neither of the magic bullets from either ideological extreme will do anything meaningful to solve that problem.

So where do we go from here? First, we need to get out of the ideological "echo chambers" we have been living in and start talking to each other. There is growing support for "doing something" about health care in the United States, but not much agreement on what that "something" might be. We are going to need a lot more consensus than we presently have, and that is going to be found in the middle rather than the edge of our political spectrum.

We are going to have to attack a problem that many members of the policy community suggest is next to impossible, and that is to transform the way the health care delivery system operates. There are a lot of entrenched interests that recognize that we have problems but are also afraid of changes. One of the most common pieces of accepted wisdom in the health policy community is that everyone's *second* option for health care reform is the status quo. Because the various first options are in conflict with each other, nobody can agree and nothing winds up happening. This is hardly a "consumer centered" system, but nothing is likely to change without a strong push from the people most affected by the current stalemate—average Americans trying to cope with a broken health care system.

What we need is a means of solving the problems that face us in a way that is minimally threatening to as many of health care's constituencies as possible, while still helping to move us toward a much more consumer-friendly system. In other words, we need to get as close as we can to a solution where everybody wins something and any pain gets spread around fairly evenly. There is no question that getting to such a solution will not be quick or cheap. One of the most common pieces of folklore says "there is never time to do it right, but there is always time to do it over." For the past half century, we have had a series of "do overs" that have not worked. Isn't it time to try "doing it right"—at least once?

Is Health Care a Right or a Privilege?

This is one of the big questions posed at the end of the first chapter. The United States is just about the only place in the developed world where this is a question worthy of debate. In most of Europe and Japan, societies are in general agreement that health care is a right, and this is shown by the near universal coverage that they provide in various forms. Even the 1948 Charter for the United Nations made reference to a right to receive medical care. In the United States, a combination of our tendency toward individualism and concern about "big government" has meant that we are still discussing the question long after it was settled in the rest of the developed world. If we really want to put consumers at the center of the health care system, the way we do so ought to be guided by what consumers think about the most important question. Let us review what various public opinion polls have had to say on the subject over the past several years.

Perhaps the most direct insight into this question comes from a Harris Interactive/*Wall Street Journal* poll conducted in October, 2003. The survey found that 65% of respondents believed that health care should be more of an entitlement, while only 23% thought it should be more of a private-market good. Not surprisingly, there were considerable differences by party affiliation. Democrats and independents both tended to support the idea that health care was an entitlement, Republicans were split just about evenly. Additional sources suggest that consumers' views on this topic have apparently remained stable for decades.

Other research and survey work have also addressed at least some aspects of this question. As this is written in late 2007, we are already seeing a number of polls tracking attitudes toward candidates and issues in preparation for the 2008 elections. The Kaiser Family Foundation's October 2007 poll indicates health care is the second most important issue overall for voters, trailing only the Iraq War. While it is not too surprising that this would be true among Democrats, this poll states that health care is also the second most important issue for independents and even Republicans. The issue has been gaining momentum across the political spectrum for the past year. The Kaiser poll identified one difference between the political parties. Republicans tended to view health care costs as the single biggest health-related issue, while coverage was the leading concern for Democrats.

Republicans have traditionally resisted the concept of health care as a "right" because of the implications it would have on the size of government. However, in June 2007 a poll of 2,000 self-described Republicans found that 51% believed that universal health care coverage should be a guaranteed right of every American. For even a slim majority of this traditionally conservative constituency to express such a view suggests that an even larger percentage of all Americans hold similar views.

The existence of programs such as Medicare and Medicaid also support the view that Americans consider health care a right, at least for some groups of people. If views of Americans are relatively close to the views expressed by Europeans, why is the U.S. health care system so different from those we see in other economically developed nations?

The short answer to this question is taxes. Residents of most major European nations face marginal tax rates that are at least 10% higher than those seen in the United States. The difference is largely accounted for by the social safety net programs common in Europe, and a very large portion of that is health care. It is relatively easy to support the idea of universal health insurance as an abstract concept. However, if the question is presented as a real-world trade-off between relatively low tax rates and health insurance for all, it becomes much more challenging. Even in Europe, there have been increasing problems maintaining the social safety net, especially for health care. As we have seen, health care costs are an increasing proportion of gross domestic product (GDP) all over the developed world, which means that, to support an equivalent amount of health care for everyone, a publicly funded system would have to raise taxes every year—not a popular option in any major country.

As a result, what we need to do is to refine the initial question a bit. People seem to support the right to some level of health care for everyone, but providing all the health care anyone could wish for at public expense is an economic nonstarter. This brings us back to the two basic methods of rationing health care (supply side and demand side) we discussed in the first chapter.

Since neither supply-side nor demand-side rationing are perfect tools, what we are starting to see across much of the developed world is a blend of both. In the United States, public-sector programs such as Medicare continue to expand as a proportion of all health care spending. In Europe, we see almost the opposite happening. Because of the economic strains these systems face, private insurance is becoming more popular for the well-to-do who would like to purchase more health care than their publicly funded system makes available, or to be able to access that care more quickly.

So, what conclusions can we draw? There is considerable support everywhere for the concept of health care as a right rather than a privilege, but that support is actually conditional. Everyone should be able to access some level of basic health care, but that almost certainly does not include a blank check for all the care anyone might suggest as possibly having some benefit. As we have seen, consumers probably are not equipped to make that choice alone, and adding to their financial exposure through high deductibles and copayments is not likely to make them smarter. As we saw in Chapter 2, the current U.S. health care delivery system is a deck stacked against them, because most of the issues that make health care more expensive here than in other parts of the world are outside their ability to easily control. This is hardly the consumer directed system most would probably like to see. If we want our health care system to be truly consumer directed, a good place to start would be to respect the views of the majority of them. This is less about some ideological concept of fairness than it is about practicality. It is going to be very difficult to get the mass of consumers to adopt a health care reform that does not fit their needs. That is what markets are all about. However, we must also meet their needs in a way that is economically sensible. We need some significant changes to our health care system if we are to achieve these somewhat conflicting goals. If that sounds like a colossal task, let me suggest a simple metaphor that might help give us a path to follow. Just as most people use their two eyes to navigate through their world, the health care system is also based on two "I's"—*information* and *incentives*. If we want health care to navigate differently, if we want to respond to consumers' views that health care is a right, but we want to do so in a way that society can afford, then these are the problems we need to attack.

Health Care Information Technology

"You cannot manage what you cannot measure." This quote is variously attributed to management gurus such as W. Edwards Demming or Peter Drucker. No matter who actually said it, it absolutely applies to health care today. As we discussed in Chapter 3, what information we have today largely comes from the claims data collected by managed care and the payer community. That information is reasonably helpful for measuring the costs of care. What we do not have is very much data on the quality of health care. The reason for this problem is simple. Somewhere between 75% and 85% of U.S. physicians still rely on paper medical charts, and even those who have electronic data usually are unable to augment it with data from other sources (such as the local pharmacy) or share the data they have with others who need to see it. If we are going to have a truly consumer-centered health care system in the United States, this has to change.

Before we can really empower anyone in the U.S. health care system, we need a significant program to bring health care's information technology (IT) capabilities up to the levels seen in other "information-heavy" industries. This means that we should be thinking seriously about solving two problems—getting more clinical data collected electronically, then making sure that data can be aggregated, analyzed, and shared with relevant stakeholders. That is the reason health care information technology (HIT) comes first on our list—because without it, few of the other changes we need to make are going to be possible.

Healthcare IT provides benefits at both an operational and a strategic level, and both are critically important. At the operational, doctor/patient level HIT helps to ensure that a physician has all the information he or she needs to diagnose and treat a patient effectively. It helps avoid the need for duplicative testing, it helps to prevent physicians from prescribing drugs that will interact with each other, and it ensures that all the providers involved with a patient's care can understand what each other are doing. This means care will be safer, better coordinated, more efficient, and more effective. At the strategic level, having access to the de-identified population-level treatment information for millions of people is critical to understanding which providers offer higher clinical quality and do so efficiently. As we will see a bit later on, this information will be critical for helping us understand the appropriate role for new technology, as well as assisting with changing economic incentives for practically every stakeholder in the health care system.

If that sounds too good to be true, there are at least two independent analyses that help to support the conclusions. In the fall of 2005, RAND completed an analysis of the value of HIT to the U.S. health care system. Their results were published in *Health Affairs*. Using very conservative criteria, these researchers cited a constellation of benefits for the entire health care system and suggested that savings of more than $81 billion per year, after paying for the roughly $120 billion cost of installing and the annual $8 billion or so needed to maintain the system, were possible. The authors further suggested that savings could be much higher if we achieved better care coordination as a result. The Center for Information Technology Leadership looked at the benefits of interoperability and also concluded building the systems to exchange electronic health care information would save the United States roughly $80 billion per year. If this is such a good idea, why have we not done it already?

The first challenge in getting the technology infrastructure we need involves getting physicians to acquire and use interoperable electronic health records (EHR). These would replace the paper charts so common today. The "interoperable" part means that the data developed in one system can be shared with others. The challenges to accomplishing this are formidable. Although prices have started to decline as innovative new business models enter the market, it still costs an average physician roughly $30,000 to purchase an EHR, and perhaps 10% to 15% of that amount each year in ongoing maintenance costs. This is a particularly difficult financial burden for physicians in "small practice" settings—one or two physicians working together.

To make matters worse, a considerable proportion of the benefit that comes from using an EHR does not accrue to the doctors who purchase them, but rather to other stakeholders in the health care system, especially consumers and third-party payers. There is also a "learning curve" effect that requires physicians to work more slowly during the initial phases of deploying an EHR. As a result, putting such a tool in place not only costs the physician the out-of-pocket purchase and maintenance costs, it also has the potential to reduce incomes while the doctor learns to incorporate the new tool into his or her practice.

The second challenge involves being able to share electronic information between sites of care. Beginning in 2003, the federal government became active in HIT, recognizing the important role this tool would have in helping to reform health care. Subsequently, a number of states have also begun to take steps to encourage the use of HIT. One of the key roles both levels of government have identified is the development of health information exchanges (HIEs) through which patient data generated at all sites of care can be aggregated into a single medical history and shared with the patient's health care providers.

According to the eHealth Initiative, there are over 100 such exchanges in development across the country, and a few have reached the stage where they can actually exchange data. Unfortunately, there have also been some high-profile failures among HIE projects during the past eighteen months, and these have begun to raise serious questions about the viability of the approach. At a national level, the U.S. Department of Health and Human Services commissioned four pilot projects to help construct a National Health Information Network (NHIN). If completed, this would allow patients' data to follow them anywhere in the country where they might require medical care. Progress, though, has been relatively slow. One of the important foundations of all federal government work in HIT and most state government activity as well has been a reliance on the private sector to do most of the work in putting the actual infrastructure in place.

In his 2005 article in *Health Affairs* entitled "Dot-Gov: Market Failure and the Creation of a National Health Information Technology System," the noted futurist J. D. Kleinke made the case that health care is not like other areas of economic enterprise, where the deployment of information technology and information sharing has been a natural activity. Kleinke noted that, if it had been in the private sector's interest to have an interoperable HIT architecture in place, it would have built it many years ago. Kleinke contrasted health care with the financial services industry and noted that an easy flow of information in health care can actually result in a loss of revenue for health care providers, since they can no longer bill for duplicating lab tests or imaging studies that exist elsewhere in the health care system but are inaccessible due to poor information flows.

What we have is a vicious cycle. Real consumer-centric health care is probably impossible to achieve without data on cost and quality. That data will not be available without a significant upgrade to the country's HIT infrastructure. However, if providers build that architecture themselves, they stand a reasonable chance of losing money as a result. The bottom line—very little happens in this critical area.

While it seems contradictory to suggest that advocates of a consumer directed health care should favor a larger role for government, there does not seem to be an easy way to break this logjam without some help from that level. Application of some financial "carrots and sticks" might offer a way out of the current dilemma. For example, as the largest health care payer in the United States, the Centers for Medicare & Medicaid Services (CMS) stands to benefit more than any other entity from the deployment of HIT, yet there have been only minimal financial incentives coming from the federal level to encourage its use. At the same time, CMS could also require the use of an EHR as a precondition for physicians to be allowed to treat Medicare patients. It seems reasonable for CMS to be talking with other members of the payer community on how they might combine their collective influence to provide economic support for the provider community to adopt HIT. "Jawboning" providers is never going to work. Neither will we get the job done by tinkering around the edges with small pilot programs or tax incentives for providers who automate. It is past time for some real investment in this space. To paraphrase the tag line of a famous athletic equipment manufacturer—"just do it."

There is another vicious cycle in HIT, and this one involves patients. There has been growing resistance to the deployment of HIT based on concerns about the privacy and security of medical information. At the same time, we clearly also have concerns about health care costs. Throughout this book we have talked about tradeoffs, and this is another one that we must think about. There is a clear relationship between health care costs, the efficiency with which care is delivered, the safety of care, and HIT. What we often hear from privacy advocates is that the risk of misuse of health care information, particularly with respect to medical insurability, is simply too great to allow the collection and sharing even of information that has been stripped of personally identifying characteristics. We cannot have it both ways, but we never seem to talk about both sides of this question at the same time.

The evidence pretty strongly tells us that health care will be more effective, better coordinated, safer, and maybe even somewhat cheaper if it is documented electronically—all of which are huge benefits for patients. So how do we get patients to cooperate? How about some new incentives? Why not tell patients they can opt out of having their care documented electronically, but that they would also be required to pay a substantially higher amount for their care in exchange for the privilege? A similar sort of penalty/reward system could be applied if patients are unwilling to allow their de-identified data to be aggregated at a population level and shared with researchers who work to try to improve the way in which the U.S. health care system operates.

The folks in the "privacy above all" community often cite very legitimate concerns that basically come down to two fundamental issues—embarrassment or discrimination. We already have laws sufficient to protect against the first; all we need to do is enforce them. The second often comes down to one word—insurability. In our current system, the sort of transparent information we are describing would represent an almost irresistible temptation for insurers to use it as a means of improving their "medical redlining" skills, thereby making the problem of uninsurance in the United States far worse, especially for people who need coverage. Rather than use this very real issue as a barrier to getting the HIT architecture we need, let us look for another way to meet that challenge, and one that will be required if we ever hope to have an individual insurance market in the United States. We will talk about this next.

Before we leave the subject of HIT, though, we need to talk about one last point. The challenges we have described in making HIT a reality sound impossible to address. However, in other parts of the world, they have already been addressed successfully. It is often said that in solving a problem, half the battle lies in knowing there is a solution at all. Parts of Europe, especially Scandinavia, have "wired" their health care systems and in many cases even built exchanges so that providers could share information to better coordinate care. In the United Kingdom, the vast majority of general practitioners now have EHRs and deliver better care at least partly because they use this technology. There are lessons we can and should learn from these other nations as we struggle with the challenges of implementing HIT here in the United States.

Community Rating, Risk Pooling, and Universal Participation

Right now, most people get coverage through either their employment or one of the two major government programs, Medicare or Medicaid. One of the reasons these group buyers are so important is that they pool the risks of many lives so that the effects of a few people who suffer very expensive illnesses in the course of a year get washed out. That is the risk-pooling concept we have discussed before. The reason it is important has to do with how insurance is sold in the United States today. One of the goals of many people in the United States is to divorce insurance from employment. While this would help to fix some of the problems associated with coverage, one of the real problems with an individual insurance market is how to ensure that people who actually need insurance are able to purchase it. To explain the cure for this issue, we need to talk a short detour into the world of insurance underwriting.

There are two fundamental ways insurance can be sold—"experience rating" and "community rating." Understanding the differences between these two will help to explain the tradeoffs involved and the challenges we must address in order to have a true consumer directed health care system.

If you buy car insurance, you are often buying an experience-rated policy. We all know and accept that individuals with worse driving records should pay more for their car insurance, while better drivers should pay less. That is exactly how experience rating works in all forms of insurance—high risks pay more, while low risks pay less. This works pretty well for auto insurance, because we generally accept that driving a car is a privilege rather than a necessity. When this system is applied to health care—something most people view as a right—a significant problem emerges. As we have already said, if you live long enough, you are likely to become a consumer of health care. In addition, while your driving record is mostly under your control, significant elements of your health (and your need for health care) are not. Obviously, a number of health issues have lifestyle components to them, such as smoking and lung cancer or obesity and diabetes. However, other forces are also at work, such as genetics and your ability to access the medical care delivery system when problems are simple to fix. As we have also already seen, age is also a significant factor. Experience rating has the effect of making health insurance extremely expensive for exactly the people who actually need it, even if the reasons for their poor health are not under their control.

Community rating for insurance works differently. In this system, everyone in a given area pays essentially the same rate for whatever insurance they are purchasing. The obvious concern with this approach is the "moral hazard" problem we discussed previously. If I have insurance at a price identical to that paid by my neighbor, do I have sufficient incentive to avoid whatever bad event I am insured against? In health care, this means that there would not be any insurance premium differentials for people who take good care of themselves versus those who do not. From an insurance company's perspective, community rating means that the firm is at the mercy of whoever chooses to sign up with them. If they happen to attract a relatively healthy batch of members, they will do well financially. However, if the luck of the draw goes against them, they cannot raise premiums to make up for the costs of providing medical care and face the prospect of a serious financial loss.

Like just about every other question we have discussed, this one involves tradeoffs and choices. The managed-care backlash of the mid-to-late 1990s meant that health insurance companies were no longer as able to manage the health care resources consumed by their enrollees. As a result, since that time, health insurance companies have largely shifted from managing care to making their profits by ensuring that they hold the "right" risk. That means offering insurance to people who are part of very large risk pools (like a large employer) or to individuals who are sufficiently healthy that they are unlikely to need any substantial amount of health care. This is good business practice, but it does have the appearance of being unfair to a number of vulnerable people in our society. It results in situations such as "job lock," where an employee who suffers from a medical condition (or has a family member who does) is unable to leave his or her job because health insurance would not be available or affordable through other means. It also means that people who do buy policies in the individual market see their premiums escalate significantly if they happen to become ill. On the other hand, simply forcing insurance companies to offer fixed rates for health insurance to all comers without some other form of compensation exposes them to the potential for a disastrous financial loss.

So what is the right thing to do?

There clearly are not any simple answers to this complex question, but some of the answers probably lie in making better use of the information technology architecture discussed above. Like the United States, the Netherlands uses a private insurance system to provide coverage. However, in the Dutch system, insurers receive a "risk equalization" payment for insuring patients who are demonstrably sicker than average. This could clearly reduce the incentives U.S. insurers currently have to "cherry-pick" healthy individuals. To make such payments truly equitable, though, we would need to have much better insight into the health of potential beneficiaries. The claims data we have in abundance at the present time is probably not sufficient to make such a determination. To get a full picture will require widespread collection of clinical data via tools like EHRs and the blending of that information with claims information via the health information exchanges discussed previously. This could begin to allow the sort of redistribution of premium dollars that would allow health insurance to be much more consumer friendly, while at the same time allowing private insurers to have confidence in accepting enrollees of varying health status.

This approach removes incentives for insurers to discriminate against people who are sick, and would therefore really help to address the privacy concerns about building the HIT architecture we discussed before. In fact, depending upon how well the risk adjustment payment was calculated, it might even become a motivator that would encourage insurers to cover people with illnesses, especially if they were also encouraged to innovate in improving the delivery of care.

We could go even further, although it would be very controversial to do so. We might want to develop a series of "carrots and sticks" for insurers to help guarantee that we get the behavior we want. For example, we could offer insurers a payment based on the severity of a beneficiary's illness with an opportunity to keep any savings they are able to generate by improving a patient's clinical outcome. At the same time, we could make the practice of "experience rating" health insurance a criminal rather than a civil offense. In other words, instead of just paying a fine for charging different premiums to people because of differences in health status, executives in a company that did so would go to jail.

Universal participation is another fix that would help insurance companies (and everybody else as well). In other words, we need mandatory purchase of health insurance for all Americans. The discussion we had in Chapter 3 about cross subsidies helps to explain why this is so important. If you recall we talked about how many people were needed to pay premiums and collect no benefits in order to support one person who was actually sick. While the demographics of the uninsured population have been changing in recent years due to the skyrocketing costs of health insurance, one group has been consistent in its tendency not to purchase health insurance, the young and healthy. Sometimes this is due to costs, other times to a belief that "I am not going to get sick, so I do not have to buy insurance." The net result is that a lot of premium payments get subtracted from the total dollars available to pay for care.

Requiring people to purchase health insurance may sound very heavy-handed. However, there is a virtuous circle that gets created if we do so. The more dollars that come as premium payments, the more affordable coverage gets for everyone. In addition, if people know that the cross subsidy they pay for at age 30 will be there to benefit them when they turn 60, it becomes a good deal easier to accept—pay now, and benefit eventually. There are also a number of precedents, things we make people do because it is simply in everyone's best interests. Mandatory purchase of auto insurance is one example. Even though we know some number of people drive without insurance, it is a crime to do so, and you are punished if you are caught. School taxes are another example. In most places property owners must pay to support their local school system whether they have children enrolled or not. If we really want health care to be affordable and accessible to all, then this is one time when the rights of the many have to trump the rights of the individual.

Provider Payment Reform

As long as physicians have their current productivity-driven economic incentives, making the health care delivery system truly patient/consumer centric will be very difficult. We have already discussed the problem of information asymmetry between doctors and patients. Once you decide to enter the health care delivery system, the physician's superior knowledge about what you need takes over and becomes the primary driving force behind what sorts of services you will actually receive. We could try to send 300 million Americans to medical school to close the knowledge gap, but it is easier to change the way doctors get paid.

This is not meant as criticism of physicians. They did not create the payment system they live in today. Like just about everything else in the U.S. health care system, it was a historical accident. Physicians spend hundreds of thousands of dollars getting their training. The overhead costs associated with a medical practice are considerable; like most of the rest of us, physicians also like to be able to feed their families. However, we have also seen that the current system provides considerable incentives for physicians to provide more services to patients, and the fact that they will be paid more if they do so does not help the problem.

As we discussed in Chapter 2, there have been experiments, mostly unsuccessful, with other ways to pay physicians, such as capitation. What most people really want from their doctors is to be kept as healthy as possible. Unfortunately, because of problems with measuring clinical outcomes, it has not been possible to give doctors the sort of financial incentives that would encourage that result. One of the benefits of the IT system described above is that it will finally allow for exactly the sorts of measurements that would make a shift to "health-focused" reimbursement a good deal more practical.

One criticism often made of paying for outcomes comes from the physicians who say that they do not know how their patients behave outside of the office and that they have no control over patient actions. There is certainly some truth to that objection; it does take two to make the doctor–patient relationship work. There is also a potential danger that, if physicians feel that their pay is dependent on patient behavior, they will refuse to treat some patients who they believe might be difficult to work with or with behavior problems that might limit their willingness to accept the physician's recommendations.

Part of the solution for this problem goes back to IT. In ambulatory care, one of the most important interventions doctors can use is prescription drugs. One prominent physician once said that primary care consisted largely of referrals, "laying on of hands," and prescribing. Unfortunately when a physician writes a prescription for a patient today he/she has no knowledge of what the patient did with that prescription. Was it ever filled? Was it consumed? Was it refilled? The physician is left with asking these questions of patients on the next office visit. Because patients seldom want to disappoint their doctors, they are inclined to tell the physician what he/she wants to hear even if it is not true. In the IT system we need to make health care more consumer centered, information from the pharmacy about prescription filling and refilling behavior would be digital and made available to physicians so that, rather than the current situation, the physician would have much better knowledge of what the patient actually did with respect to prescribed medication and could have a productive conversation with that patient if such medication use was not what is required.

The other part of the fix is to change patient financial incentives as well. We will talk about this in more detail a bit later on, but by modifying the "blunt instrument" nature of the current copayment structure of "version 1" CDHPs, it should be possible to create a shared set of incentives that can reinforce the doctor–patient relationship.

So what sort of new compensation program might be possible? At present, there are somewhere in the range of 150 documented "pay-for-performance" programs in the United States, but many agree that these efforts are still in their infancy. As with any infant, there are "growing pains" involved, reflected in a number of interesting questions surrounding pay for performance at the present time.

What is "performance?" Currently, because we lack most of the information we really need to measure outcomes, many pay-for-performance programs track process measures. For example, the doctor is graded on whether or not certain tests were performed. As long as the process being measured is well correlated with a good clinical outcome, this is not a bad thing. In a more problematic version, physicians are paid "quality" bonuses for treating patients inexpensively. For example, bonus dollars are allocated for prescribing generic drugs even if the patient's case suggests the use of a more expensive branded product might be a better clinical choice. Clearly, we once again come back to the critical need for better IT to help with at least parts of this problem.

How is "performance" defined? There are at least three ways to do this, and each has is own plusses and minuses. The easiest method is to target the overall percentage of times the physician achieved the desired goal. For example, if the objective is to screen all diabetics for potential eye problems, and a physician can document this was done 90% of the time, then 90% of available bonus dollars for that measure are paid out. Obviously the metrics have to be selected carefully so that they represent something important yet achievable. Otherwise a physician can become very frustrated with an unattainable goal. A second, slightly more complex method is to reward improvement over time. With this technique, everyone has a chance to "win," but there is some risk that, unless the improvement thresholds are defined carefully, the bonus will be either too hard or too easy to earn. The final and most complex method is a bit like the "grading on a curve" system used in some schools. This approach rewards only the best performers against a certain metric. At first glance this sounds appealing, but it has problems. The "zero-sum" nature of the competition means that only some physicians can win. This tactic also leaves much to be desired if the goal is not just to reward the best performers, but to improve the performance of all physicians.

Finally, how much is paid for "performance?" Most current programs have fairly modest potential payouts for physicians, generally less than 5% of total compensation. Given the potential for a number of competing programs, all with different metrics, this simply is not enough money to provide incentives for most physicians to change their behavior. If performance bonuses could be raised to 10% to 20% of total compensation, the motivation for physicians to do the extra work required probably increases enough to produce the desired behavior. Unfortunately, this leads to yet another problem—is the bonus to be paid for performance simply a redistribution of existing compensation, or does it represent new money on top of what is already being paid? Physicians can view the former as a "takeaway," hardly what we want if we are interested in motivating them to act differently. However, the latter just fuels the problem we are trying to solve in the first place—more money being spent on health care than we believe we can afford.

These may sound like academic issues, but they are not. Getting this right, and getting the medical community's support is absolutely critical to changing the perverse physician incentives that are such a significant contributor to health care spending differences between the United States and the rest of the developed world. As difficult as these issues are, the temptation might be to try "blunt instrument" tools like simply cutting physician compensation across the board. However, this approach is likely to have even worse consequences, because it would certainly not provide the sorts of incentives to encourage our "best and brightest" to consider medical careers or to encourage those physicians already working to try to improve.

Another part of the fix almost certainly includes focusing physicians more on the work that only they can do. This will involve making greater use of what are variously called "physician extenders" or "midlevel providers" such as physician's assistants, nurse practitioners, and pharmacists. There is considerable evidence that the use of extended care teams involving a more varied mix of medical professionals improves the overall quality of care. It would have the additional benefit of helping to optimize the use of physician time, one of the most expensive resources in the health care delivery system. Extending the number of professionals involved in care delivery creates its own problems, mostly involving communication and coordination of activities. Once again, an important part of the solution for this challenge lies in the "wiring" of American medicine so that health care providers can communicate with each other at least as well as can employees in any other modern industry.

Once again, there are some lessons we can learn from other nations. The United Kingdom's National Health Service implemented a very large pay-for-performance program a few years ago, plowing a considerable amount of new money into the system. Reports on this program suggest that nearly all benchmarks originally set by the National Health Service were met or exceeded. While there is still some debate about precisely how these goals were achieved, there is little doubt that the quality of care received by most U.K. National Health Service patients has been very good. We could do worse than to look at this program and see what elements we might want to use here as we attempt to change the economic incentives for our clinicians.

Modified Consumer Financial Incentives

One of the biggest concerns about current CDHPs is where the financial incentives and penalties lie, because these do have a profound effect on consumer behavior. As we have already seen, the bulk of medical costs are concentrated in the care of a relatively small number of people. Even if we assume that 100% of Americans were enrolled in CDHPs, this concentration of health spending means that once these individuals had spent their way through their deductible, they would become cost-insensitive consumers for the rest of their care during that year. Raising the patient's cost-sharing burden to the point where it would be a significant influence on behavior would make care for these individuals unaffordable.

The RAND Health Insurance Experiment and most of the early experience with current consumer directed plans shows that consumers do cut back on the use of care that is subject to cost sharing. Unfortunately, they appear to reduce needed and unneeded care in equal proportions. We know that the vast majority of medical spending is associated with chronic disease, and most experts believe that treating such diseases correctly in their early stages can prevent or at least defer the development of expensive complications later on. This raises an obvious question about the incentives in current consumer directed plans. While many plans do provide "safe harbors" that dispense with copayments for preventative care, it seems clear that exempting management of chronic disease from cost-sharing burdens that would discourage patients from visiting their doctors for recommended follow-up care or taking their medications would be a logical extension. In other words, patients with chronic disease should not be subjected to copayments for their physician visits, drugs, or required laboratory tests.

We have also seen that health literacy in the United States is a major problem, limiting consumers' ability to make good decisions. To make matters worse, we have also seen that consumers suffer from not having the sort information available to them that would allow any sort of reasonable decision making that would weigh cost versus real medical quality. Until the IT architecture is completed, this situation is not likely to improve. Therefore, if we want people to be better decision makers, we need to make it much easier for average consumers to make good decisions. This means more fundamental changes to the design of health insurance benefits.

Perhaps the best example of making it easy for consumers to make good decisions comes from a very different part of the world—financial services and retirement planning. What has happened in this field over the past thirty years contains some useful lessons for health care.

In 1978, Congress passed the Revenue Act, which contained a provision that fundamentally changed the way in which retirements were funded. Over the course of the succeeding three decades, more and more workers lost their "defined-benefit" pensions—fully funded by employers with payments for life. In exchange, the new plans, referred to as "defined-contribution" vehicles, were called 401(k)s after the section number of the portion of the Revenue Act that created them. These new plans shifted the burden for savings and for deciding how these savings would be invested to individual workers. Such plans also often offer a matching company contribution based on the percentage of wages the worker saves, and they usually also offer a large variety of potential investment vehicles.

What has happened over the past thirty years? Unfortunately, we have learned that a number of consumers have not been especially good decision makers. A 2005 study done for the consulting firm Hewitt by academic economists from Harvard and the University of Pennsylvania found that 39% of employees did not participate in their firm's 401(k) plan at all, despite the fact that this was often the only retirement plan offered to them. Fully 40% of participants did not save enough money in their 401(k) plan to even maximize their employer's matching contribution. Another study, done in 2004 by the investment firm Vanguard, found that many enrollees in 401(k) plans were not particularly astute about investing their contributions. Thirteen percent of participants had their entire balances invested in fixed income securities, and 25% had more than 20% of their balances invested in the stock of their employers—both considered to be serious errors by financial professionals.

Employers have a strong vested interest in addressing these problems. If employees are able to amass sufficient assets to provide for a comfortable retirement, they are more likely to be willing to leave work at the appropriate point in their careers. As a result, employers have recently started to take action to correct these problems. Recent changes to the laws that govern 401(k) plans have allowed employers to make these plans "opt-out" instead of "opt-in." In other words, instead of relying upon employees to take the active step of enrolling in a retirement plan, employers can now legally automatically enroll employees unless they are proactive in informing their employer otherwise. Just implementing this simple step can double plan participation rates. Employers have also been simplifying investment decision making. According the a report prepared for AARP in June 2007, the consulting firm Tower-Perrin found that 81% of all 401(k) plans offered more than ten different investment choices, with more than a quarter offering twenty or more investment options. Psychologists have shown that "decision overload" is a serious problem for many people. In the face of seemingly limitless choices, people often tend to choose "none of the above," frozen by the complexity facing them. The new trend is not just to autoenroll employees in their firm's 401(k) plan, but to also "autoselect" an investment option for them. These are often "lifecycle" funds that invest in a mix of assets based on the target retirement year of the participants. Such funds are not necessarily the perfect investment option, but tend to be reasonably good for most people. Employees are always free to change the allocation of their investments as they choose. In other words, employers have learned the hard way that consumers need a good deal of help in making correct decisions. As a result, what employers are now doing is making it much easier for employees to do the right thing, and much harder for them to do the wrong thing.

Health care is at least as complicated as financial planning, and many people would probably say it is more complicated due to the specialized knowledge required. If large enough numbers of consumers have been consistently unable to manage their retirement planning "correctly" over a course of nearly thirty years such that their employers feel the need to simplify the process, it seems likely that, if we want a consumer-centered health care system, we are going to need something similar. We have already mentioned one of the findings from the October 2007 Fidelity Investments survey, but this study also found that 68% of insured workers had not even tried to calculate their expected health care costs for retirement, and only 10% had carefully estimated the amount of savings they would need to cover these costs. Harris Interactive's Strategic Health Perspectives survey found similar results. Only 5% of baby boomers correctly estimated that they would need $250,000 or more to pay for out-of-pocket medical expenses in retirement, and when asked if they would have enough saved to cover this amount, 73% said it was "not at all likely" they would have done so.

Over the course of the past year, we have actually started to see the first indications that employers are starting to apply the difficult lessons learned from helping employees fund their retirement to the design of health benefits. The National Business Group on Health is a coalition of some of the nation's largest and most sophisticated employers. This group's members are responsible for most of the cutting-edge thinking with regard to employer-sponsored health care in the United States. Much of the agenda for the group's March 2007 meeting was devoted to a new topic—"value-based benefit design." Many of the most interested parties were firms that had been early implementers of first-generation consumer directed health care plans. In brief, value-based benefit design attempts to customize the menu of benefits offered and the required cost sharing based on the overall value of the medical intervention concerned. What the most vocal proponents of value-based benefit design would like to see is evaluations of all sorts of medical interventions and the providers who offer them. Ideally, this sort of evidence base could then be applied against a particular employee's medical history so that any financial cost sharing could be used to "channel" that employee to interventions best suited for his or her personal situation and to physicians who have a track record of delivering those interventions in a high-quality, timely, and cost-efficient manner. In other words, employees would pay less to use products and services that are documented to provide better outcomes and would pay less if they got those services from "better" providers. Although employees would always have the right to "opt out" of these default choices, if they chose other interventions or providers they would have to finance a higher proportion of the costs with their own money.

There is a philosophy named "libertarian paternalism" that describes how this sort of approach works. If you have ever helped to educate a child, teach someone else a skill, or even train a pet you might recognize what underpins this thinking. "Make it easy to do the right thing" is one of the first principles of success in all these activities, and that is what we need to do for the next generation of consumer directed health care. While we never want to remove a consumer's right to select a form of care or a provider of his or her choice, we do want to ensure that the default options are ones that are unlikely to lead to a bad result.

How could this work in practice? Let us assume a person has just enrolled in a "version 2" consumer directed health plan. As he signs up for his policy, he is directed to a listing of primary care physicians who practice within ten miles of his home. The first thing the new enrollee notices is the required copayment. Two of the five physicians show zero copayment, while the other three show a $20 copayment. Reading further, he finds that the two "zero-copay" doctors have been found to provide higher quality care at a lower total cost than his other three options. He likewise finds that the medications he needs to keep his blood pressure under control will be available to him at no cost as long as he continues to refill his prescriptions every month and visit his doctor at regular intervals for follow-up care. He also reads that, if he fails to do these things and suffers a cardiac event as a consequence, he will be liable for the first $5,000 of his hospital bill.

While this is a grossly simplified example, the message is clear. Financial incentives are used to channel consumers into making choices that are clearly in their best interests as well as the best interests of society. The consumer still maintains the right to ignore the guidelines and do as he or she pleases; however, if something bad happens as a result of that choice, the consumer will face significant economic consequences.

Of course, this leads to the critical question of who gets to decide what health services are preferred and how that decision is make. We will take up that question right after we talk about some needed changes to health savings accounts (HSAs).

Improving the Health Savings Account

One of the best ideas associated with the first generation of CDHPs is encouraging consumers to save money for their later health care expenses. We have already discussed the out-of-pocket retirement health care spending estimates made by groups like EBRI and Fidelity Investments. Providing extra incentives to encourage consumers to accumulate as much money as possible in vehicles like HSAs can only help them to deal with these challenges. Unfortunately, today, to obtain the potential benefits of an HSA, a consumer also needs to enroll in a high-deductible health plan, which comes with its own set of potential problems and, as we have seen, is not particularly popular with average consumers. One way to address this problem is to uncouple the HSA from the high-deductible plan so that consumers could have access to the long-term benefits of the savings vehicle without having to also accept the more problematic insurance plan.

One of the criticisms leveled at HSAs is that they only provide substantial tax advantages for individuals in higher tax brackets. According to the Internal Revenue Service, in 2005, there were about 91.5 million tax returns filed. About 3.5 million of these reported taxable income of over $200,000, enough to reach into the 33% bracket. If we add in those with taxable incomes of $75,000 or more—enough to reach the 28% bracket, the number rises by another 21 million. Even with a fairly liberal definition of "high income" we still have less than one in three taxpayers able to extract meaningful benefit from the tax shelters offered by HSAs. Health care costs, though, will probably eventually affect everyone, regardless of income. If we are really serious about asking all people to save more money, we probably need to think about incentives that are meaningful to the 65 million taxpayers who really cannot benefit from HSAs today. This might take a number of different forms, including a dollar-for-dollar tax credit. While the budgetary impact of this would probably be considerable, if we want to encourage long-term savings for health care expenses later in life and make the HSA useful for all consumers, we are going to need to make these sorts of changes.

One of the biggest challenges with the current CDHPs is that the deductible is identical for all holders of a particular policy regardless of their income level. In real life, $1,000 to $2,000 out-of-pocket spending has a very different effect on someone earning $50,000 (close to the median household income in the United States) versus someone earning $500,000. For the one, the deductible is little more than an inconvenience; for the other, it is a serious financial burden, especially if it is an expense that is incurred year after year, as would usually be the case for a patient suffering from a chronic disease.

The Bureau of Labor Statistics publishes some very interesting data on the spending patterns of U.S. households stratified by age and by income level. It shows that the average or mean household income in 2005 was about $59,000 a year. Why is this higher than the median income cited in the last paragraph? Because there is a great deal of "skew" in distribution of income. A few people with extremely high incomes make the average higher than the median (the point at which half the households are above and half are below). For all of the 117 million "consumer units" (households) in the United States, the average out-of-pocket spending on health care is about $2,700. That represents about 4.5% of income and roughly 6% of annual household spending—which totals about $46,000 a year. Health care spending does rise somewhat with income level. You will spend about two or three times as much out-of-pocket on health care if you are in the top 20% of wage earners than if you are in the bottom 20%. However, there is a fifteen-fold spread in income between the top and bottom fifth of incomes. As a result, health care out-of-pocket spending equals 15% of income for the poorest 20% of Americans, but less than 3% for the wealthiest 20%.

This rapidly growing gap between health care spending and income has made the underinsurance problem we discussed in Chapter 3 a good deal more acute. Unfortunately, lower-income households who enroll in the current generation of consumer directed plans are also at risk. This is probably one of the reasons consumers do not voluntarily select these plans more often when they have a choice of insurance coverage.

We have already seen the effect age has on total health care spending. It has a somewhat similar effect on out-of-pocket spending as well. If you are under 25, your health care spending will average about $700. That represents about 2.5% of average income. By the time you are between 55 to 64 years of age, your out-of-pocket health care spending will rise to about $3,400. Your income will have risen as well, to about $64,000. In other words, out-of-pocket health care spending will consume about 5% of your income.

One way to address this problem would be to tie the cap on out-of-pocket spending in a high-deductible plan to income. Admittedly this would make administering these plans a great deal more complex, but if our goal is a patient-centered health care system with more people enrolling in consumer directed plans, it is what is needed. If we also make the suggested adjustments to the deductible to exclude the costs of chronic disease therapy from patient cost-sharing requirements, that will also help considerably. If the second generation of consumer directed plans ensures that no one in the United States pays more than 5% of household income on health care, and that enrollees will not have to pay anything out-of-pocket for preventative or maintenance care, we would remove many of the disincentives to seek needed care that are present in the current CDHPs. Restructuring CDHPs this way will still provide incentives for consumers to be cost conscious for the more expensive elements of their care while ensuring that no one suffers a catastrophic loss as a consequence of a health problem.

A final potential option for both making heath care more affordable yet still encouraging consumers to be active in their care would blend this goal with our earlier theme of "make it easy for consumers to do the right thing" by tying at least some out-of-pocket costs to the consumer's own behavior. For example, if a chronic disease patient visited his physician as recommended, took medication as prescribed, and did the other medically necessary things to manage his/her condition, perhaps that patient should face much lower out-of-pocket costs for those services than a patient who was not as compliant. This is not unlike the sort of "safe driver" discounts offered for car insurance today, and would be a logical extension of the exemptions common in the first generation of consumer directed plans for preventative care. Such discounts would be offered from the community-rated premium that we discussed previously, but if we believe what the medical literature tells us about the ability of relatively simple medical interventions like physician visits and regular use of prescribed medication to save the health care system money while also improving the quality of patients' lives, it is the right thing to do. Such an approach has the additional benefit of reducing some of the objections from the medical community to the "pay-for-outcomes" approach to physician compensation we discussed before. In this approach, the physician's incentives and the patient's incentives are very closely aligned and should strengthen the critical relationship between the two.

Technology Assessment and Comparative Effectiveness Reviews

We have talked about a health care IT infrastructure and the information it can generate. Unfortunately, information does not interpret itself; someone has to do that and make decisions as a result. In the "version 2" of consumer directed health care we are describing, those decisions will have broad implications for what providers are preferred, what technologies those providers will be able to use, and what services will be financially advantaged for CDHP enrollees. Some people have suggested that technology assessment can be conducted independent of evaluating the quality of physicians. The problem with that approach is that, in many cases, it is very hard to separate the two. For example, even if we have an excellent joint replacement it is hard to achieve a superior clinical outcome if the orthopedic surgeon does not do a good job. The challenges of evaluating technology are somewhat different from those we see with evaluating physicians, so we will look at that part of the equation first.

In Chapter 2, we saw that one of the important drivers of U.S. health care costs was open access to technology. New devices, diagnostics, and drugs are readily available in this country after they prove basic safety and effectiveness to the satisfaction of the Food and Drug Administration (FDA)—the federal agency that regulates these industries. It is generally not required for such new products to document that they are better than what is available today—something we commonly see in much of the rest of the developed world. New technology is a double-edged sword though. Yes, it contributes to health care costs, but it also gives providers new tools to use to cure disease, restore lost functions, and improve the quality of life. Without technology, providers are often helpless in the face of illness. Putting up high barriers to all new technology would certainly reduce health care costs, but at a price few people would be willing to pay.

What we need is a system that evaluates innovative products in health care quickly and fairly, while providing sufficient incentives for product developers to invent new technologies that improve the quality of care at an appropriate cost to the system. The process by which new drugs and devices get approved for use in the United States is conducted in a very tightly controlled environment. This is necessary to allow the FDA to determine whether or not they work and are safe. Unfortunately, this process does not tell us much about how new technologies will perform in real-world settings that are far less controlled. As a result, it is very difficult to make a determination about the actual value such products bring to patients from the information generated during the time they are being studied prior to approval.

Getting the information we need is not easy, but once again, part of the answer comes back to HIT. Here is how it might work. During the time a new product is in development the innovator works to build an outcomes case, the best way it can given the constraints of the regulatory process. When the product is finally approved for sale, if the case the innovator has created provides a reasonable presumption of value, the product receives conditional reimbursement—meaning it gets paid for while the product gets used in more realistic settings. After some period, perhaps six months, perhaps twelve months, data concerning the product's performance are extracted from the national HIT network and analyzed to see if the product has actually performed as expected. That data can be further examined to determine if there are certain types of patients for whom the new product is a better (or worse) choice than available alternatives. The reimbursement for the product is then adjusted at regular intervals to reflect the ongoing process of collecting and analyzing data.

This is similar to the process we will need to use to determine which providers do a better job of treating patients, so the mechanics of how it is structured and administered are very important. As we discussed in Chapter 2, we have made some previous and mostly unsuccessful attempts to regulate the flow of new technology entering the U.S. market. In many cases, the reason these attempts failed is that one stakeholder (often a payer) set itself up as judge and jury in an "I win/you lose" game with technology developers. If we are going to have a process that is strong and durable enough for the difficult task at hand, we will have to do it differently in the future.

So who decides? There is no perfect answer to this question because there is no group, body, or agency that does not have a bias of some kind. Payers are obviously interested in making care as inexpensive as possible; technology developers want wide access to markets; providers want as much decision-making latitude as possible; and the list goes on. Since there are no truly independent decision makers, the only answer is to include all the constituencies in the process. Federal and state governments, employers, insurers, physicians, hospitals, pharmaceutical manufacturers, medical device companies, diagnostic developers, nurses, pharmacists, and others need a seat at this table.

There are already a number of organizations that are attempting to measure medical quality on behalf of one or more of health care's stakeholders. It is quite possible that one of these could serve as the convening body for these constituencies to meet and deliberate. A number of important questions about the mechanics of the evaluation process remain, and there are tradeoffs for each one of these.

- Should this be a government-centered process, or should the process be dominated by the private sector? A large government footprint ensures that the process will get the appropriate attention from health care's other stakeholders. On the other hand, would such a role represent more intrusion into health care than average Americans want to see from government?
- Should there be a single national-level quality/effectiveness review process, or should there be several (possibly at a regional, state, or local level)? A single process would be a clean "all or nothing" for technology innovators, and preparing for a single evaluation with a single set of standards would make the process simpler for those whose products or skills are being evaluated. On the other hand, health care tends to be a local/regional process, and there are legitimate concerns about how responsive a single national process could be to local issues.
- Should actual payment/reimbursement decisions be tied to the measurement and evaluation process, or should the two be separate? A process linking the two would ensure the relevance of the evaluation effort, but would the spending pressures on health care create too great a temptation to make the process mostly about unit costs rather than true value? If the two are not linked, then who does take responsibility for actually negotiating prices with providers and technology suppliers? Is this something that insurers will do, or is it up to individual consumers? How can we ensure that this activity is fair to all concerned?

These are not simple questions, and a number of individuals in the health policy community are devoting a lot of effort to getting them sorted out. Because they will have such a great impact on the future of health care, it is useful for all of us to at least understand the issues and develop a point of view.

So, what have we learned about "version 2" of consumer directed health care? It revolves around incentives and information. First, we need to spend time and money building an HIT architecture. If that does not happen, we have little hope of getting to a sustainable health care system, especially one that is consumer centered. We also need to revamp the way insurance is sold to remove the current perverse incentives to "cherry-pick" healthier enrollees and to give us a reasonable basis for a market that focuses more on individuals than the current employer-sponsored large group policies. We also need to fix provider incentives by paying for outcomes rather than activity. This will also help with the "information asymmetry" problem. We need to look at how to simplify consumer decision making by changing their incentives as well. This will help to make certain that the interests of doctors and patients are aligned. We need to make HSAs more accessible to average Americans, and we need to cap the amount of money a family can spend out-of-pocket on health care annually. Finally, we need a collaborative process to evaluate technology and measure the quality of providers. Then we can truly say we have got a system of delivering health care that is not only consumer centered but prepared for the challenges we will face over the next half century.

Perhaps the easiest way to summarize what I believe the next version of consumer directed health care should look like is by giving you one last personal analogy. My father has been a music lover throughout his life. He played trumpet in his youth and was one of the early adopters of what was once the newest technology—stereo. In the early 1960s, he worked with some friends to draw up plans for a pair of speakers he wanted to have so that he could enjoy his music fully. These speakers were quite large—perhaps three feet tall, almost two feet wide, and about two feet deep as well. I remember my father carefully cutting up the wood to make the enclosures and assembling them. I remember him putting the speakers in these enclosures and soldering the connections. When he was done, he had two very nice pieces of furniture that fulfilled his need for a better way to play his music. The combination of his skill with both wood and electronics, along with his passion for good sound blended to allow him to do something extraordinary.

I guess the love for music must be hereditary, because it is an interest of mine as well. Over the years, I have spent more money than I would care to admit on various black boxes, cables, and speakers. In order to get everything to work together, I needed to do a lot of research and experimentation. However, the one thing I could never do with my home sound system was take my music with me when I traveled. For a number of years, I resisted buying a portable MP3 player because I was not sure about how much I would enjoy the sound quality. However, at the urging of friends I broke down this year and purchased one of the new iPods™ from Apple. These devices are technological marvels. Right out of the box, they are set up to do exactly what most consumers want—play music. The connection to the computer is extraordinarily simple, and it is also very easy to either load your own CDs onto the device or purchase songs. While there are a great many settings on my iPod that I have learned to tweak, the defaults built into the device worked just fine. This device is a bit larger than a credit card, but it is durable, portable, and lets me carry around almost two thousand songs that I can listen to whenever I have some spare time.

What has this got to do with consumer directed health care? Where we are today is probably comparable to the situation my father faced in the 1960s. It was possible to get good sound, but he needed to be really interested in the area and also have a reasonable degree of sophistication about electronics and woodworking as well. Likewise, it is possible for at least some individual consumers to successfully navigate through the health care system today, but it requires a great deal of interest and skill. In contrast, when I bought my iPod, I did not really need to know much about the technology inside, I simply paid my money and got pretty good performance without having to apply a lot of effort. The advanced technology is all there, but it works almost invisibly to let me do what I want, without requiring that I have an engineering degree or significant computer programming skills. That is what we need to do with health care. All our knowledge of medical science and finance should be combined to give consumers something that works for them without them having to necessarily understand the inner workings of the system. Obviously, we will still need to give consumers the ability to modify any sort of basic program we develop. Choice still matters, because one size never really does quite fit everyone. However, consumers who do not have the aptitude or the ability to get into the details of their health insurance should have a default option that does not require them to so do. When we have done that, when the system is as easy to operate as my iPod, we will know that we have achieved "version 2" of consumer directed health care.

Alternatives

If you have read this chapter and are thinking "this is a *lot* of work," you are absolutely right. Nothing that we have talked about will be quick, cheap, or easy. There is a natural temptation to just try to "muddle through" and defer the painful decisions for another time. So why not just roll over, hit the snooze alarm, and leave it all to somebody else to handle?

The answer to that question takes us back to the first two chapters of the book. The health care problems we face are getting greater by the day. We face an explosive mix of baby boomers who are starting to roll out of the workforce without either good health insurance coverage or enough money to purchase it on their own. Employers see health care costs going up at twice the rate of other business expenses (if they are lucky) and taking larger bites out of the income statement. We are looking at trillions of dollars in unfunded liabilities in Medicare, and the number is getting bigger every day we delay. Every fix we have tried so far has been useful, but unable to stem the tide—and that includes the first generation of CDHPs. Getting consumers involved in health care is a great idea, but turning the existing mess we call a delivery system over to them and asking them to sort it out is a recipe for failure. Combine an increasing number of people who cannot access the system at all with an increasing number who are confused and unable to make good choices in the health plan they have, and we get a large enough number of people to create a political wave. At that point, the only option might be a course of action that few want—having the government step in to sort the mess out with price controls, radically higher tax rates, and "bare bones" coverage.

If you think that is too bleak a picture of our future, let me add one last data point from the Harris Interactive work. The firm asked a variety of stakeholders who should be responsible for making sure that all Americans have health care. Over half of each segment of the general public, and almost two-thirds of baby boomers responded that it was the federal government's job to do so. Even a majority of physicians supported the federal government as the agency primarily responsible for the task. In contrast, only about a quarter of the audiences surveyed believed it was the responsibility of individuals. Perhaps this is just another reflection of "health care as a right or a privilege" question, or maybe it is a recognition of the problems consumers face trying to cope with today's health care market. Either way, it suggests a much larger government footprint if things do not change.

That is not a pretty picture, especially since we can still do something about it. I hope you are willing to roll up your sleeves, get informed, and help with the hard but necessary work we have ahead of us. The hour is late, but we can still make a difference if we decide to do so. The choice is yours.

Epilogue

If this book has helped to make you a better-informed participant in the big debates we are having, and will continue to have, about health care, then I am happy. Some of you may be curious about where various bits of information I have included came from. Others of you may be interested enough in what you have read that you would like to learn more.

Getting educated on health care and health policy really is not that difficult it you want to make an effort to so do. The list of "recommended reading" you will find next represent most of the source material I used in preparing this book. A high percentage of these references are available over the Internet at no cost. You just have to go look for them. I have made several references to *Health Affairs* in the book, and a number of articles published in that journal are included on my reading list. These are sources that require you to purchase them. However, if you have any lasting interest in health care and health policy, I would recommend you buy a subscription. *Health Affairs* is probably the most informative publication you can read, and it is not particularly expensive. If you work for a health care organization of some sort, and you can afford to spend five figures in an effort to better understand what is going on in health care, I would also recommend that you think seriously about subscribing to Harris Interactive's Strategic Health Perspectives service. I have used a great deal of their data in this book, but there are literally hundreds of pages of very useful information available for subscribers, and it is interpreted by some of the smartest people in health care.

I hope you have enjoyed reading this book as much as I have enjoyed writing it. Most importantly, I hope I have left you more knowledgeable for the experience and more prepared to join with the other 300 million people who have a stake in health care to ensure that we get a real consumer directed system.

Recommended Reading

AHIP. January 2007 census shows 4.5 million people covered by HSA/high deductible health plans. America's Health Insurance Plans, Center for Policy and Research, April 2007. http://www.ahipresearch.org/PDFs/FINAL%20AHIP_HSAReport.pdf (accessed February 15, 2008).

Anderson, Gerald F., Peter S. Hussey, Bianca K. Frogner, and Hugh R. Waters. Health spending in the United States and the rest of the industrialized world. *Health Affairs* 24(4): 903–914, 2005.

Anderson, Gerard F., Uwe E. Reinhardt, Peter S. Hussey, and Varduhl Petrosyan. It's the prices, stupid: Why the United States is so different from other countries. *Health Affairs* 22(3): 89–105, 2003.

Appleby, Julie. Even the insured have trouble paying bills. *USA Today*, March 22, 2007.

Appleby, Julie. People left holding the bag when policies revoked. *USA Today*, January 29, 2007.

Audet, Anne-Marie, Karen Davis, and Stephen Schoenbaum. Adoption of patient centered care practices by physicians. *Archives of Internal Medicine* 166: 754–759, 2006.

Banks, James, Michael Marmot, Zoe Oldfield, and James P. Smith. Disease and disadvantage in the U.S. and in England. *Journal of the American Medical Association* 295(17): 2037–2045, 2006.

Becker, S. A. Web accessibility for older adults. Northern Arizona University, 2003. http://cob.fit.edu/facultysites/abecker/Accessibility/Readability/WebReadability.html (accessed February 15, 2008).

Berenson, Alex. Sending back the doctor's bill. *New York Times*, July 29, 2007.

Blumenthal, David. Employer-sponsored health insurance in the United States— Origins and implications. *New England Journal of Medicine* 355: 82–88, 2006.

Buntin, Melinda Beeuwkes, Cheryl Damberg, Amelia Haviland, Kanika Kapur, Nicole Lurie, Roland McDevitt, and M. Susam Marquis. Consumer directed health care: Early evidence about effects on cost and quality. *Health Affairs* 25(6) (Web Exclusive): w516–w530, 2006.

California Health Care Foundation. Designing coverage: Uninsured Californians weigh the options. California Health Care Foundation, June 2007. http://www.chcf.org/documents/insurance/DesignCoverageForUninsured.pdf (accessed February 15, 2008).

Chu, Kathy. Employers get creative to get workers to participate in 401(k)s. *USA Today*, August 9, 2006.

CIGNA Corporation. Cigna Consumer Choice Fund Experience Study: Summary of key findings. CIGNA Corporation, October 2007. http://www.cigna.com (accessed February 15, 2008).

Collins, Sara R., Kathy Schoen, Karen Davis, Anne K. Gauthier, and Steven C. Schoenbaum. A roadmap to health insurance for all: Principles for reform. The Commonwealth Fund, October, 2007. http://www.commonwealthfund.org/usr_doc/Collins_roadmaphltinsforall_1066.pdf?section=4039 (accessed February 15, 2008).

Congressional Budget Office. Consumer-directed health plans: Potential effects on health care spending and outcomes. Congressional Budget Office, Pub. No. 2585, December 2006. http://www.cbo.gov (accessed February 15, 2008).

Decker, William F. Medical savings accounts: Fact sheet. AARP, May 2000. http://www.aarp.org/research/health/carefinancing/aresearch-import-683-FS80.html#What (accessed February 15, 2008).

Diamond Management & Technology Consultants. Competitive implications of consumer-directed health care. Goldman Sachs and Diamond Management & Technology Consultants, September 28, 2006. http://diamondconsultants.com/PublicSite/ideas/perspectives/downloads/INSIGHT%20-%20Diamond%20and%20Goldman%20Sachs%20CDHS%20Recap%20-%209_26_06.pdf (accessed February 15, 2008).

Fabrizio, McLaughlin & Associates. The elephant looks in the mirror 10 years later: A critical look at today's Grand Old Party. Fabrizio, McLaughlin & Associates, Inc., June 2007.

Fidelity Investments. Fidelity research reveals many insured U.S. workers don't understand basic consumer health plan language. *Business Wire*, October 16, 2007. http://www.fidelity.com (accessed February 15, 2008).

Fronstin, Paul and Sara R. Collins. The 2nd Annual EBRI/Commonwealth Fund Consumerism in Health Care Survey, 2006: Early experience with high-deductible and consumer-driven health plans. Employee Benefit Research Institute Issue Brief 300, December 2006. http://www.commonwealthfund.org/usr_doc/IB-Dec06-Final-E-CF-Logos.pdf?section=4039 (accessed February 15, 2008).

Gabel, Jon, Jeremy Pikreign, and Heidi Whitmore. Behind the slow enrollment growth of employer-based consumer-directed health plans. Center for Studying Health System Change Tracking Report, Number 107, December 2006. http://www.hschange.com/CONTENT/900/?topic=topic01 (accessed February 15, 2008).

Girion, Lisa. Health insurer tied bonuses to dropping sick policyholders. *Los Angeles Times*, November 9, 2007.

Gladwell, Malcolm. The moral hazard myth. *New Yorker* August 29, 2005.

Goldman, Dana P., Geoffrey F. Joyce, and Yuhui Zheng. Prescription drug cost sharing, associations with medication and medical utilization and spending and health. *Journal of the American Medical Association* 298(1): 61–69, 2007

Gross, Daniel. 911 for 401(k)s: Why we're so incredibly stupid about retirement investing. *Slate*, March 1, 2005. http://www.slate.com/id/2114196/ (accessed February 15, 2008).

Gruber, Jonathan. The role of consumer copayments for health care: Lessons from the RAND Health Insurance Experiment and beyond. The Henry J. Kaiser Family Foundation, October, 2006. http://www.kff.org/insurance/upload/7566.pdf (accessed February 15, 2008).

Helman, Ruth, Jack VanDerhei, and Craig Copeland. The retirement system in transition: The 2007 Retirement Confidence Survey. Employee Benefits Research Institute, Issue Brief 304, April 2007. http://www.ebri.org/pdf/briefspdf/EBRI_IB_04a-20075.pdf (accessed February 15, 2008).

Herick, Devon M. Medical tourism: Global competition in health care. National Center for Policy Analysis, Report #304, November 2007. http://www.ncpa.org/pub/st/st304 (accessed February 15, 2008).

Hillestad, Richard, James Bigelow, Anthony Bower, Federico Girosi, Robin Meili, Richard Scoville, and Roger Taylor. Can electronic medical record systems transform health care? Potential health benefits, savings and costs. *Health Affairs* 24(5): 1103–1117, 2005.

Himmelstein, David U., Elizabeth Warren, Deborah Thorne, and Steffie Woolhandler. Illness and injury as contributors to bankruptcy. *Health Affairs* 25 (Web Exclusive): W5-63–W5-73, 2005.

Horowitz, Michael D., Jeffrey A. Rosensweig, and Christopher A. Jones. Medical tourism: Globalization of the healthcare marketplace. Medscape General Medicine, November 13, 2007. http://www.medscape.com/viewarticle/564406_1 (accessed February 15, 2008).

Hsiao, William C. Why is a systemic view of health financing necessary? *Health Affairs* 26(4): 950–961, 2007.

Institute of Medicine. Health literacy: A prescription to end confusion. Institute of Medicine of the National Academies, Report Brief, April 2004. http://www.iom.edu/Object.File/Master/19/726/health%20literacy%20final.pdf (accessed February 15, 2008).

Jacobs, Michael and Wayne M. Lednar. Consumer-directed health plans: Built to last or designed to fail? A point–counterpoint debate with Michael Jacobs RPh, and Wayne M. Lednar, MD, PhD. *Managed Care* 16(8): 41–47, 2007. http://www.managedcaremag.com/archives/0708/0708.counterpoint.html (accessed February 15, 2008).

Jacobson, Peter D. and Michael R. Tunick. Consumer-directed health care and the courts: Let the buyer (and seller) beware. *Health Affairs* 26(3): 704–714, 2007.

Kahn, James G., Richard Kronick, Mary Kreger, and David Gans. The cost of health insurance administration in California: Estimates for physicians, insurers, and hospitals. *Health Affairs* 24(6): 1629–1639, 2005.

Kaiser Family Foundation. National survey of enrollees in consumer directed health plans. Kaiser Family Foundation, November, 2006. http://www.kff.org/kaiserpolls/pomr112906pkg.cfm (accessed February 15, 2008).

Kaiser Family Foundation. Health care costs: A primer, key information on health care costs and their impact. Kaiser Family Foundation, August, 2007. http://www.kff. org/insurance/upload/7670.pdf (accessed February 15, 2008).

Kaiser Family Foundation. Kaiser Health Tracking Poll: Election 2008, Issue 4, October 2007, Kaiser Family Foundation, 2007. http://www.kff.org/kaiserpolls/ h08_pomr102607pkg.cfm (accessed February 15, 2008).

Kaiser Family Foundation and Health Research Educational Trust. Employer Health Benefits, 2007 Annual Survey. Kaiser Family Foundation and Health Research Educational Trust, 2007. http://www.kff.org/insurance/7672/upload/76723.pdf (accessed February 15, 2008).

Kim, Minah, Bobert Blendon, and John Benson. How interested are Americans in new medical technologies? A multicountry comparison. *Health Affairs* 20(5): 194–201, 2001.

Kleinke, J. D. Dot-gov: Market failure and the creation of a national health information technology system. *Health Affairs* 24(5): 1246–1262, 2005.

Kulka, Rebecca. How do patients know? *Hastings Center Report* 37(5): 27–35, 2007. http://www.medscape.com/viewarticle/563286 (accessed February 15, 2008).

Leach, Howard. Consumer directed health plans: Testimony of Howard Leach, head of human resources, Logan Aluminum, Inc., before the Joint Economic Committee of the U.S. Congress, February 25, 2004. http://www.aetna.com/about/aoti/ business_solutions/logan_testimony.html (accessed February 15, 2008).

Lee, Christopher. Health insurance's new wave and the man behind the plans. *Washington Post*, December 28, 2006, A25.

Liebhaber, Allison and Joy M. Grossman. Physicians moving to mid-sized, single-specialty practices. Center for Studying Health System Change Tracking Report Number 18, August 2007. http://www.hschange.com/CONTENT/941/ (accessed February 15, 2008).

McCarrick, Pat Milmoe. A right to health care. National Reference Center for Bioethics Literature, Georgetown University. Scope Note 20, 1992. http://bioethics.george-town.edu/publications/scopenotes/sn20.pdf (accessed February 15, 2008).

McGlynn, Elizabeth A., Steven F. Asch, John Adams, Jennifer Hicks, Alison DiChrisofaro, and Eve A. Kerr. The quality of health care delivered to adults in the United States. *New England Journal of Medicine* 348(26): 2635–2645, 2003.

McKinsey Global Institute. Accounting for the cost of health care in the United States. McKinsey Global Institute. January 2007.

Miller, Harold D. Creating payment systems to accelerate value-driven health care: Issues and options for policy reform. The Commonwealth Fund, September, 2007. http://www.commonwealthfund.org/publications/publications_show. htm?doc_id=522583 (accessed February 15, 2008).

Milstein, Arnold and Mark Smith. Will the surgical world become flat? *Health Affairs* 26(1): 137–141, 2007.

Naik, Gutam. In Holland, some see model for U.S. health care system. *Wall Street Journal*, September 6, 2007, A1.

National Center for Policy Analysis. Brief history of health savings accounts. National Center for Policy Analysis, NCPA Brief Analysis No. 481, 2004. http://ncpa.org (accessed February 15, 2008).

National Health Care Anti-Fraud Association. Health care fraud: A serious and costly reality for all Americans. National Health Care Anti-Fraud Association, April 2005. http://www.nhcaa.org (accessed February 15, 2008).

Newhouse, Joseph P. Consumer-directed health plans and the RAND Health Insurance Experiment. *Health Affairs* 23(6): 107–113, 2004.

Peters, Ellen, Judith Hibbard, Paul Slovic, and Nathan Dieckmann. Numeracy skill and the communication, comprehension, and use of risk-benefit information. *Health Affairs* 26(3): 741–748, 2007.

Peterson, Chris L. and Rachel Burton. CRS Report for Congress—U.S. Health Care Spending: Comparison with Other OECD Countries (RL34175). Congressional Research Service, September 17, 2007. http://www.opencrs.com/rpts/RL34175_20070917.pdf (accessed February 15, 2008).

Pham, Hoangmi P., Kelly J. Devers, Jessica H. May, and Robert Berenson. Financial pressures spur physician entrepreneurialism. *Health Affairs* 23(2): 70–81, 2004.

RAND Corporation. Consumer directed health plans: Implications for health care quality and cost. California Health Care Foundation, June 2005. http://www.chcf.org/documents/insurance/ConsumerDirHealthPlansQualityCost.pdf (accessed February 15, 2008).

RAND Corporation. The Health Insurance Experiment, A classic RAND study speaks to the current health care reform debate. Rand Corporation. 2006. http://www.rand.org/pubs/research_briefs/2006/RAND_RB9174.pdf (accessed February 15, 2008).

RAND Corporation. Consumer-directed health care: Early evidence shows lower costs, mixed effects on quality of care. RAND Corporation, 2007. http://www.rand.org/pubs/research_briefs/2007/RAND_RB9234.pdf (accessed February 15, 2008).

Reinhardt, Uwe E. Does the aging of the population really drive the demand for health care? *Health Affairs* 22(6): 27–39, 2003.

Rudd, Rima, Irwin Kirsch, and Kentaro Yamamoto. Literacy and health in America. Educational Testing Service, 2004. http://www.ets.org/Media/Research/pdf/PICHEATH.pdf (accessed February 15, 2008).

Serota, Scott. The individual market: A delicate balance. *Health Affairs* Web Exclusive: w377–w379, October 23, 2002.

Shaller Consulting. Consumers in health care: Creating decision-support tools that work. California Health Care Foundation, June 2006. http://www.chcf.org (accessed February 15, 2008).

Shapiro, Robert Y. and John T. Young. The polls: Medical care in the United States. *Public Opinion Quarterly* 50(3): 418–428, 1986.

Smith, Sheila. The macro picture: Medical innovation and growth in health care costs. Health Care Financing Administration (HCFA), The National Academies Board on Science, Technology and Economic Policy, Technological Innovation in a Changing Medical Marketplace, June 14, 2001. http://www7.nationalacademies.org/step/Smith_presentation.ppt (accessed February 15, 2008).

Taylor, Humphrey and Robert Lietman (Eds.). Widespread pessimism: Large majority thinks health care system will get worse—Large majority also sees health care more as an entitlement than a private economic good. *Health Care News* 3(16), October 27, 2003. http://www.harrisinteractive.com/news/newsletters/healthnews/HI_HealthCareNews2003Vol3_Iss16.pdf (accessed February 15, 2008).

Thorpe, Kenneth E., David H. Howard, and Katya Galactinova. Difference in disease prevalence as a source of the U.S.–European health care spending gap. *Health Affairs* 26 (Web Exclusive): w678–w686, 2007.

Towers-Perrin. Enhancing 401(k) value and participation—Taking the automatic approach—A report for AARP prepared by Towers-Perrin. AARP, June 2007. http://assets.aarp.org/rgcenter/econ/enhancing_401k.pdf (accessed February 15, 2008).

Trust for America's Health. F as in fat: How obesity policies are failing in America. Trust for America's Health, 2007. http://www.healthyamericans.org (accessed February 15, 2008).

Tu, Ha T. and Paul Ginsberg. Losing ground: Physician income 1995–2003. Center for Studying Health System Change, Tracking Report, No. 15, June 2006.

U.S. Bureau of Labor Statistics. Consumer Expenditures In 2005. U.S. Department of Labor, U.S. Bureau of Labor Statistics, Report 998, February, 2007. http://www.bls.gov/cex/csxann05.pdf (accessed February 15, 2008).

Van Deusen, Allison. Outsourcing your health. *Forbes*, May 29, 2007. http://www.forbes.com/business/2007/05/21/outsourcing-medical-tourism-biz-cx_avd_0529medtourism.html (accessed February 15, 2008).

Wallace, Lorraine Silver and Elizabeth S. Lennon. American Academy of Family Physicians patient education materials: Can patients read them? *Family Medicine* 36(8): 571–574, 2004. http://www.stfm.org/fmhub/fm2004/September/Lorraine571.pdf (accessed February 15, 2008).

Woolhandler, Steffie and David U. Himmelstein. Paying for national health insurance, and not getting it. *Health Affairs* 21(4): 88–98, 2002.

World Health Organization. 2007. *World Health Statistics 2007.* Geneva: World Health Organization, 2007. http://www.who.org (accessed February 15, 2008).

Index

About the Author

Kim D. Slocum is President of KDS Consulting, LLC, an organization devoted to helping stakeholders in health care develop strategic, sustainable solutions to the challenges they face. He has almost thirty-five years working in U.S. health care. Before founding KDS Consulting in 2006, he had been employed by a number of life sciences firms in a variety of roles. For the past fifteen years he has focused his attention primarily on issues related to health care strategy, policy, and economics, and these remain his passions today. He is a fellow member of the Healthcare Information and Management Systems Society (HIMSS) and former member of the society's board of directors. He is also an emeritus member of the board of trustees of the Texas Health Institute and a senior scholar at the Thomas Jefferson Department of Health Policy in Philadelphia. He is affiliated with Harris Interactive's Strategic Health Perspectives service. He is also a frequent speaker and author on issues related to health care. He earned his bachelor's degree from the State University of New York at Geneseo in 1971 and did his graduate studies in business at Xavier University. He was born in upstate New York and currently lives in West Chester, Pennsylvania, with his wife and two cats.